YORK NOTES

General Editors: Professor A.N. Jeffares (*University of Stirling*) & Professor Suheil Bushrui (*American University of Beirut*)

William Shakespeare

TWELFTH NIGHT

Notes by Loreto Todd

MA (BELFAST) MA PHD (LEEDS)
Senior Lecturer in English, University of Leeds

 LONGMAN
YORK PRESS

YORK PRESS
Immeuble Esseily, Place Riad Solh, Beirut.

LONGMAN GROUP UK LIMITED
Longman House, Burnt Mill, Harlow,
Essex CM20 2JE, England
Associated companies, branches and representatives
throughout the world

First published 1980
Eighth impression 1990

ISBN 0-582-02316-5

Produced by Longman Group (FE) Ltd.
Printed in Hong Kong

Contents

Part 1

Introduction

The Elizabethan age

Queen Elizabeth I came to the throne in 1558 and ruled England until 1603. Her reign brought stability to the country and with stability came prosperity. In order to see how important peace and order were to the Elizabethans, it is useful to contrast Elizabeth's reign with the insecurity and unrest of earlier ages.

Historical background

Elizabeth's grandfather, Henry Tudor, became King Henry VII of England in 1485. His accession and subsequent marriage to Elizabeth of York put an end to the Civil Wars which had racked England for almost a hundred years. Henry VII concentrated on reducing friction at home and abroad and on establishing a strong, financially secure monarchy.

He was succeeded in 1509 by his son Henry VIII who married a Spanish princess, Catherine of Aragon. This marriage did not produce a son and so Henry VIII divorced her. The divorce was condemned by the Catholic Church and, gradually, a split developed between the Pope and Henry. Henry died in 1547 and at that time England was still largely a Catholic country, Catholic, that is, in practice, though the supreme spiritual authority of the Pope had been challenged, and many Protestant reformers were eager to spread Protestantism in England.

Henry VIII was succeeded by his nine-year-old son Edward and his Regents furthered the spread of Protestantism. Edward died in 1553 and was followed to the throne by his half-sister Mary, daughter of Catherine of Aragon and a devout Catholic. She attempted to restore Catholicism to England but she too died childless and was succeeded in 1558 by her Protestant half-sister Elizabeth.

Elizabeth adopted what might be called a 'middle way' course as far as religion was concerned. She broke the link with Rome but retained many of the practices and beliefs of the old religion. Her 'middle way' satisfied most of her subjects and for the majority of her reign religious strife was avoided. Many different Christian sects became established in England during her reign, however, among them the Puritans who are referred to in *Twelfth Night* (see Act II, Scene 3, 140–153).

Social background

In spite of the political and religious turmoil of the reigns prior to Elizabeth's, most Elizabethans were convinced that they lived in an ordered universe, a universe in which God was supreme and in which angels, men, animals, plants and stones had their allotted place. The Christian view that mankind was redeemed by Christ was rarely challenged by Elizabethans though points of detail might be argued about. In spite of the teaching that Adam's fall had, to some extent, spoiled God's plans for mankind, there was a widely held belief in universal order and harmony. The stars and the planets were still in accord with the divine plan and it was believed that they gave glory to God by the music of their movement. Shakespeare expresses this idea in *The Merchant of Venice* when Lorenzo tells Jessica:

> Look how the floor of heaven
> Is thick inlaid with patines of bright gold;
> There's not the smallest orb which thou behold'st
> But in his motion like an angel sings,
> Still quiring to the young-ey'd cherubins;
> Such harmony is in immortal souls,
> But whilst this muddy vesture of decay
> Doth grossly close it in, we cannot hear it.
> (V.1.58–65)

Before Adam's fall man too could hear the heavenly harmonies. Although the fall put an end to this ideal state the heavenly bodies continued to influence life on earth. Just as the Sun gave warmth and light, just as the Moon caused the tidal movement of the seas, so too did the stars and planets affect the earth and its inhabitants. Most Elizabethans attributed certain types of behaviour to astrological causes such as one's birth sign, or the relative position of the planets at a particular time. Some people even believed that individual parts of the body were under the control of specific planets or constellations. There is evidence of such belief in Act I of *Twelfth Night* where the following conversation takes place between Sir Toby Belch and Sir Andrew Aguecheek:

SIR TOBY: I did think by the excellent constitution of thy leg, it was formed under the star of a galliard.
SIR ANDREW: Ay, 'tis strong, and it does indifferent well in a flame-coloured stock. Shall we set about some revels?
SIR TOBY: What shall we do else? Were we not born under Taurus?
SIR ANDREW: Taurus? That's sides and heart.
SIR TOBY: No, sir, it is legs and thighs.
       (I.3.129–38)

Interestingly, both Sir Toby and Sir Andrew got the reference wrong. Taurus was, in orthodox astrology, associated with the neck and throat. Most of Shakespeare's audience would have realised that and they would have seen the unintentional aptness of Sir Toby's reference to Taurus. The revels enjoyed by Sir Toby and Sir Andrew involved more drinking than dancing.

The Elizabethans, like many people before and since then, were aware of man's paradoxical position in nature. He was influenced by the stars and the planets, subject to his passions and, at the same time, made in the image and likeness of God. This duality in human nature is aptly summed up by Alexander Pope (1688–1744) who described man as:

> Great lord of all things, yet a prey to all;
> Sole judge of Truth, in endless Error hurled:
> The glory, jest, and riddle of the world!
> ('Essay on Man')

Man was most in harmony with Nature and with his creator, it was believed, when his reason controlled his emotions, and a similar truth was believed to apply to the state. Natural disorders, like storms and earthquakes, were paralleled by passionate outbursts in the individual and by disputes in the state. These views are more clearly seen in such Shakespearean plays as *King Lear* and *Othello* where natural storms symbolise the turmoil and confusion of the characters, but they were commonly held in Elizabethan times. The nearest we come to the expression of such a belief in *Twelfth Night* is in the use of music. The Duke asks for it in the opening scene to help him to bear the passionate love he feels for Olivia, and it occurs again at the end of the play when mysteries have been solved and lovers united.

William Shakespeare (1564–1616)

We know very little about who Shakespeare was or how he lived. And, apart from the ideas expressed in his writings, we know nothing at all about what he thought or how he reacted to the events of his time. He was born in Stratford-upon-Avon in Warwickshire and was baptised there on 26 April 1564. His father, John Shakespeare, seems to have been reasonably wealthy at the time of William's birth. He had business interests in farming, butchering, wool-dealing and glove-making and he held several public offices in Stratford until about 1578 when his business began to decline.

It seems likely, in view of his father's position, that William was educated at the Stratford Grammar School. He did not, however, go to university and so did not have the kind of education which many contemporary playwrights experienced.

William Shakespeare married Anne Hathaway in 1582 when he was eighteen and she twenty-six and, by 1585, they had three children, Susanna, born shortly after the marriage, and twins Judith and Hamnet born in 1585. We cannot be certain how Shakespeare supported his family during this time. He may have been involved in his father's diminishing business or he may, as some traditions suggest, have been a schoolmaster. Whatever he did, however, it did not satisfy him completely because he left Stratford and went to London.

Once again, we cannot be sure when Shakespeare moved to London. It may have been in 1585, the year when a group of London players visited Stratford and performed their plays there. But we do know that he was living in London in 1592, by which time he was already known as a dramatist and an actor. Indeed, even at this early date, his plays must have been popular because, in 1592, Shakespeare was criticised in a pamphlet by a less successful writer, Robert Greene, who wrote that a new and largely uneducated dramatist (that is, Shakespeare) was usurping the position which rightly belonged to university men.

Plague broke out in London in 1593 and all theatres were closed. Shakespeare seems to have used the time of the closure to write two long poems, 'The Rape of Lucrece' and 'Venus and Adonis' and to strengthen his relationship with a theatre group called the Lord Chamberlain's Company in Elizabeth's reign and the King's Men after the accession of James I in 1603. Shakespeare maintained his association with this company until he retired from the theatre and he seems to have prospered with it.

In 1596 came personal grief and achievement. His son Hamnet died and he and his father were granted a coat of arms which meant that their status as 'gentlemen' was recognised by the College of Heralds. In the following year, 1597, Shakespeare bought New Place, one of the largest houses in Stratford. In 1599 he bought shares in the Globe Theatre and in 1609 he became part owner of the newly built Blackfriars Theatre. In this year also, he published a collection of sonnets. Shakespeare retired to New Place in 1611 though he did not break all his business contacts with London. He died in Stratford on 23 April 1616 at the age of fifty-two.

Background notes on Elizabethan drama

Records of drama in English go back to the Middle Ages, a period in which numerous 'miracle' and 'morality' plays were written. Such plays were often based on biblical themes, especially those involving miraculous events such as the saving of Noah and his family in the ark, or those from which a clear moral could be drawn. Medieval plays were usually written to coincide with such religious festivals as Christmas or Easter and they were often performed in or near the church, with most of the community taking part either actively, by playing a role, or passively, as a member of the audience.

In the medieval period drama was a significant element in the structure of society. It was, in many ways, an extension of Christian ritual and was meant to make a strong impression on all who participated in the performance. Audiences were meant to be awed by the power and wisdom of God, inspired by the faith and courage of holy men, frightened by the fate of evil-doers and amused by the folly of mankind. Drama in the period was thus meant to have a cathartic effect, that is, it was intended to improve the members of the audience by giving them an outlet for such emotions as greed, hatred, lust and pity. They were encouraged to identify with a character often called Everyman who represented all men in their journey through life. The drama of the time, like Everyman himself, had a universal appeal. It was written, not for a small élite, but with all members of the society in mind.

In the early sixteenth century the close relationship that had previously existed between Church and State began to change. Individual Christian sects had distinctly different attitudes to the role of drama in society. It was tolerated by Catholics but condemned by Puritans who wished to 'purify' the religious beliefs and attitudes and to encourage people to give up worldly pleasures so that they might attend to spiritual matters. Puritanism grew stronger, especially in towns and cities, in the second half of the sixteenth century and people connected with drama—writers and actors—had to struggle against growing opposition. Elizabethan dramatists often criticised Puritanism in their plays and there is some evidence of such criticism in *Twelfth Night* (see Character Notes—Malvolio, pp.55-7). Puritanical opposition to the theatre eventually succeeded in curtailing freedom of speech in drama when they sponsored the Licensing Act which was passed by Parliament in 1737.

In Shakespeare's day, however, the theatre had the support of the court and many dramatists, including Shakespeare, continued the medieval tradition of producing plays which appealed to all classes and to different levels of intelligence and education.

Contemporary dramatists

Numerous Englishmen wrote plays in the sixteenth century, men such as John Lyly, Thomas Kyd, Robert Greene and Thomas Nashe. Among the most talented of these dramatists was Christopher Marlowe (1564-93). He was born in the same year as Shakespeare but seems to have begun writing plays before Shakespeare did. He was a gifted poet and many of his dramatic innovations were adopted by playwrights of his own and later generations. He was the first English dramatist to make effective and extensive use of blank verse, that is, he frequently used an organised pattern of rhythm in his plays giving his verse the memorability of poetry and the effortlessness of natural speech:

> The stars move still, time runs, the clock will strike,
> The devil will come, and Faustus must be damned.
> O I'll leap up to my God: who pulls me down?
> See, see where Christ's blood streams in the firmament.
> One drop would save my soul, half a drop, ah my Christ.
>
> (*Doctor Faustus*, lines 1429–33)

THE GLOBE PLAYHOUSE

The theatre, originally built by James Burbage in 1576, was made of wood (Burbage had been trained as a carpenter). It was situated to the north of the River Thames on Shoreditch in Finsbury Fields. There was trouble with the lease of the land, and so the theatre was dismantled in 1598, and reconstructed 'in another forme' on the south side of the Thames as the Globe. Its sign is thought to have been a figure of the Greek hero Hercules carrying the globe. It was built in six months, its galleries being roofed with thatch. This caught fire in 1613 when some smouldering wadding, from a cannon used in a performance of Shakespeare's *Henry VIII*, lodged in it. The theatre was burnt down, and when it was rebuilt again on the old foundations, the galleries were roofed with tiles.

Marlowe was the forerunner of Shakespeare in that he centred his tragedies on one main character, a character with whom the audience could sympathise, but he was closer than Shakespeare to the medieval tradition in that his characters tend to behave like supernatural beings.

Shakespeare seems to have learned much from his contemporaries, especially Marlowe, and from the medieval dramatic tradition. He borrowed plots and ideas from many sources but they were transformed by his poetry and his dramatic talents.

The Elizabethan theatre

Drama became increasingly secularised during the fifteenth and sixteenth centuries and plays ceased to be performed in or near a church. Instead, they were often staged in the courtyard of an inn. Putting on a performance in such a courtyard had several advantages. There were many doors which could be used for exits and entrances, balconies which could represent battlements or towers and, best of all, perhaps, there were usually guests in the inns who were glad of entertainment.

When the first theatre was built in London, in 1576, it seemed perfectly natural, therefore, to build it according to the design of Elizabethan courtyards. The theatre had galleries and boxes around the walls where the wealthy sat and, like the courtyard of an inn, it had no roof and so performances were cancelled when the weather was bad. The 1576 theatre and those built subsequently differed from the courtyard in that they contained a large stage—often called an 'apron' stage because of its shape—which jutted out from one wall into the auditorium. The poorer members of the audience were called 'groundlings' and they stood around the stage throughout the performance.

The large apron stage was not curtained from the audience and there was no scenery on it. Indications of where the scene occurred were built into the words of the play. In Act II, Scene 3 of *Twelfth Night*, for example, Malvolio in criticising the revellers indirectly informs the audience of the time and place of the action:

> My masters, are you mad? or what are you? Have you not wit, manners, nor honesty, but to gabble like tinkers at this time of night? Do ye make an ale-house of my lady's house . . .?
> (II.3.87–90)

The lack of scenery was also, in part, compensated for by the use of very rich costumes and music.

In the sixteenth and early seventeenth centuries, it seems likely that plays went on from beginning to end without interval, though the end of a serious scene was often indicated by the use of rhyming couplets.

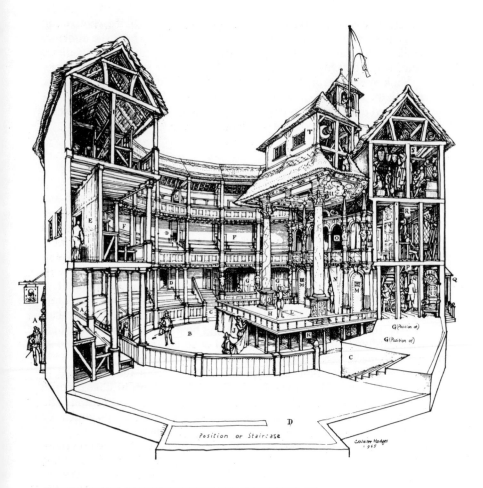

A CONJECTURAL RECONSTRUCTION OF THE INTERIOR OF
THE GLOBE PLAYHOUSE

AA Main entrance
 B The Yard
CC Entrances to lowest gallery
 D Entrance to staircase and upper galleries
 E Corridor serving the different sections of the middle gallery
 F Middle gallery ('Twopenny Rooms')
 G 'Gentlemen's Rooms' or Lords' Rooms'
 H The stage
 J The hanging being put up round the stage
 K The 'Hell' under the stage
 L The stage trap, leading down to the Hell
MM Stage doors

N Curtained 'place behind the stage'
O Gallery above the stage, used as required sometimes by musicians, sometimes by spectators, and often as part of the play
P Back-stage area (the tiring-house)
Q Tiring-house door
R Dressing-rooms
S Wardrobe and storage
T The hut housing the machine for lowering enthroned gods, etc., to the stage
U The 'Heavens'
W Hoisting the playhouse flag

In Act I of *Twelfth Night*, for instance, Scenes 1, 2, 4 and 5 are all end-rhymed:

> Away before me to sweet beds of *flowers* :
> Love-thoughts lie rich when canopied with *bowers*. (I.1.40-1)

In Shakespeare's time, women were not allowed to perform on the stage, and so female roles were played by boys. This fact helps to explain why so many of Shakespeare's heroines, heroines such as Portia in *The Merchant of Venice*, Rosalind in *As You Like It* and Viola in *Twelfth Night*, disguise themselves as young men. It was easier for a boy to act like a young man than to act like a young woman.

Elizabethan English

Every living language changes. Differences in pronunciation and in linguistic preferences are often apparent even in the speech of a father and his son, so it is not surprising that the language of Shakespeare's plays should be markedly different from the English we use today. In the sixteenth century the English language was only beginning to be used by creative writers. Previously, Latin and French had been considered more suitable for literary expression than English and consequently the English language had not been as fully developed as it might have been. Because of this the language of Shakespeare and his contemporaries is used less systematically than it is today.

Mobility of word classes

Adjectives, nouns and verbs were less rigidly confined to their specific classes in Shakespeare's day. Adjectives were often used as adverbs. In Act III, Scene 4, line 4 Olivia says: 'I speak too *loud*' where modern standard usage would require 'I speak too loudly'. Adjectives could also be used as nouns. In the same scene, lines 90-1, Malvolio tells Fabian: 'Go off, I discard you: let me enjoy my *private* : go off.' where today he would say 'privacy'.

Nouns were often used as verbs. In Act IV, Scene 2, 94, Malvolio complains of his captors: 'They have here *propertied* me; keep me in darkness', where the noun 'property' is used as if it were a verb with the meaning of 'take posession or control of'; and verbs were also, on occasion, used as nouns. In Act II, Scene 4, 102, when the Duke says:

> Make no *compare*
> Between that love a woman can bear me,
> And that I owe Olivia

'compare' is used where today we need 'comparison'.

Changes in word meanings

Words change their meanings as time passes, and so many words used by Shakespeare have different values today. Such change can be illustrated by the following examples. 'Admire' which now means 'look at with pleasure or satisfaction', 'have a high regard for', meant 'wonder at', 'be amazed' in Shakespeare's day and this is the sense in which it is used in Sir Andrew's challenge to Cesario in Act III, Scene 4, 152–3:

> Wonder not, nor admire not in thy mind, why I do call thee so, for I will show thee no reason for 't.

'Complexion' now usually refers to the natural colour of the face but in Shakespeare's writings it refers to one's total outward appearance, so when in Act II, Scene 4, 26, Viola describes the one who has won her heart as being of the Duke's 'complexion', she is referring not only to his colouring but to his appearance generally.

'Silly' meant 'simple', 'innocent' and not 'foolish'. In Act II, Scene 4, 46 when the Duke describes the words of a song he heard the previous evening as: 'it is silly sooth', he implies that it is the simple, unadorned truth.

Vocabulary loss

The occurrence of 'sooth' in the last example illustrates another difficulty in Shakespeare's language. Many words which occur in his plays are no longer current in modern English. This is true of the following items from *Twelfth Night*:

anon (V.1.47): immediately
barful (I.4.41): extremely difficult
bawcock (III.4.114): a handsome fellow
bawbling (V.1.52): trifling, worth very little, insignificant
botcher (I.5.52): a person who mended old clothes
brabble (V.1.63): fight, quarrel
cantons (I.5.294): songs
champaign (II.5.160): open countryside
coistrel (I.3.40): fellow of no repute
cozier (II.3.91): cobbler, maker of shoes
duello (III.4.314): duel
extravagancy (II.1.11): extravagance
gaskins (I.5.24): trousers, Elizabethan stockings for men
geck (V.1.342): an idiot, fool
haggard (III.1.65): a wild hawk

kickshawses (I.3.113): unimportant trifles
leman (II.3.26): beloved, sweetheart
malapert (IV.1.43): cheeky, pert
maugre (II.1.153): in spite of
misprision (I.5.53): mistake, misunderstanding
perpend (V.1.298): listen carefully, weigh the evidence
point-device (II.5.163): exactly, precisely
saw (III.4.388): wise saying, proverb
scathful (V.1.54): harmful, destructive
shent (IV.2.108): scolded
testril (II.3.34): small coin worth about 1/40 of £1
tuck (III.4.226): sword
wainropes (III.2.57): strong ropes used to tie oxen or horses to a cart
welkin (III.1.59): sky, heavens
whirligig (V.1.375): wheel, spinning top
yare (III.4.226): quick, ready
zanies (I.5.88): fools, idiots

The difficulties posed by changes of meaning and loss of vocabulary can be easily exaggerated. The majority of words that occur in Shakespeare's plays are still used today and their meanings are usually made clear by their context.

Verbs

Shakespearean verb forms differ from modern usage in three main ways. Firstly, questions and negatives could be formed without using 'do' or 'did'. Thus, in Act II, Scene 4, 120, the Duke asks Viola: '*Died* thy sister of her love?' where today one would have to say: '*Did* your sister *die* of her love?' Similarly, in Act II, Scene 3, 4, Sir Andrew Aguecheek says: '. . . I know not' using a construction which would be considered ungrammatical in modern English. One must add, however, that Shakespeare often formed questions and negatives as we do today. In Act III, Scene 4, 263, for example, Viola asks: '. . . do you know of this matter?' and in Act I, Scene 5, 187, Olivia replies: 'If I do not usurp myself, I am' to Viola's question. Whereas, however, Shakespeare could use both:

1(*a*) Like you it?	*and*	1(*b*) Do you like it?
2(*a*) I like it not	*and*	2(*b*) I do not like it
3(*a*) Liked you it?	*and*	3(*b*) Did you like it?
4(*a*) I liked it not	*and*	4(*b*) I did not like it

modern English only permits the (*b*) forms.

Secondly, some past participles are used which would be ungrammatical today. In *Twelfth Night* the following occur:

(1) 'hid' for modern 'hidden':
   Wherefore are these things *hid*? (I.3.122)
(2) 'spoke' for modern 'spoken':
   As it is *spoke* (I.4.20)
(3) 'took' for 'taken' and 'mistook' for 'mistaken':
   He might have *took* his answer long ago (I.5.267)
   Lady, you have been *mistook* (V.1.257)
(4) 'writ' for 'written':
   Twas well *writ* (III.4.38)
(5) 'forgot' for 'forgotten':
   Hast thou *forgot* thyself? (V.1.139)
(6) 'broke' for 'broken':
   He has *broke* my head across (V.1.173)

Thirdly, archaic forms of the verb sometimes occur with 'thou' and with 'he/she/it':

Know'st thou this country? (I.2.21)
He *hath* better bethought him (III.4.302–3)

but, as with other changes in the language, these are readily understood in the context of the play.

Pronouns

Shakespeare's pronoun usage differs to some extent from our own. There was a certain amount of choice in the use of second person pronouns in Elizabethan English. 'You' had to be used when addressing more than one person:

My masters are *you* mad? (II.3.87)

or when one wished to indicate respect. Thus Antonio and Sebastian show their mutual respect by addressing each other as 'you':

ANTONIO: If *you* will not murder me for my love, let me be your
            servant.
SEBASTIAN: If *you* will not undo what *you* have done, that is, kill him
            whom *you* have recovered, desire it not.
            (II.1.34–7)

Superiors used 'thou' to their inferiors and were, in return, addressed as 'you'. The Duke, for example, addresses Cesario:

Thou know'st no less but all (I.4.13)

whereas all the Duke's servants address him as 'you':

Will *you* go hunt, my lord? (I.1.16)

The use of 'thou' could indicate that one was talking to an intimate. Sir Toby frequently uses this form when speaking to Sir Andrew:

Then hadst *thou* had an excellent head of hair (I.3.94)

When used inappropriately, however, 'thou' could imply an insult. Thus when Sir Toby is encouraging Sir Andrew to challenge Cesario to a duel he says:

. . . taunt him with the licence of ink: if thou *thou*'st him some thrice, it shall not be amiss . . . [that is, if you use the 'thou' form he will be insulted and may thus accept your challenge].
(III.2.42–4)

One further pronominal difference which may be noted is the use of 'it' to refer to a person. In Act I, Scene 5, 102, Maria describes Cesario as: '. . . *'t*is a fair young man, and well attended', and in Act II, Scene 4, 26 the Duke uses 'it' where 'she' would occur in modern English: 'What kind of woman is *'t*?'

Prepositions

In Elizabethan England prepositional usage was less standardised than it is today and thus many of Shakespeare's prepositions differ from those which would be employed today. Among these are:

'of' where modern usage requires 'by':
A lady, sir, though it was said she much resembled me, was yet *of* many accounted beautiful: (II.1.24–5)

'of' for 'from':
There's a testril *of* me too (II.3.34)

'on' for 'at':
Even now, sir, *on* a moderate pace I have since arrived but hither. (II.2.2–3)

'on' for 'of':
What should I think *on*'t? (II.5.28)

'to' for 'with':
No man hath any quarrel *to* me (III.4.228–9)

Multiple negation

In modern English we use only one negative in a sentence but in Shakespeare's day two or even more negatives could be used for emphasis. In his sonnet 'Let me not to the marriage of true minds', for example, Shakespeare concludes with the following couplet:

> If this be error and upon me proved,
> I never writ, nor no man ever loved.

In *Twelfth Night* we find many examples of double negatives, among them the following:

> ANTONIO: Will you stay no longer? nor will you not that I go with
> you? (II.1.1–2)

and:

> SIR ANDREW: Nor I neither. (II.5.186)

Shakespeare's plays

Shakespeare's creative period as a dramatist spans approximately twenty years, from about 1591 until 1611. During this time he is believed to have written thirty-seven plays and he may have collaborated on the writing of a number of others. It is not always easy to know when individual plays were written but some idea of dating can be gained from records of performances, from the order given in editions of the plays published before and shortly after his death. It is on the basis of such evidence that scholars suggest 1601 as the probable date of the composition of *Twelfth Night*.

Shakespeare's plays were not 'original' in the modern sense of 'new'. Many of his plots were borrowed from history or from contemporary literature but they were moulded by him into unique and successful plays. These can be divided into two main types, comedies which had happy endings and tragedies which involved the death of the chief character.

The nature of comedy

Shakespearean comedies usually treated the happier aspects of life such as love and marriage, often, as in *Twelfth Night* making lavish use of music and singing. Frequently, there were two levels in the comedy, one involving the love interests of ladies and gentlemen and another dealing with the humorous behaviour of less elevated characters. Often the amusing scenes highlight the contrast between human aspirations and achievements. Hypocrisy and affectation are gently ridiculed, confusion and contradictions exaggerated.

Prose is used in comic scenes whereas blank verse is the usual medium for more serious interaction. By alternating between prose and poetry Shakespeare can thus emphasise differences in language and behaviour while, at the same time, implying the essential similarity between the needs and urges of all his characters and stressing too the common humanity they share with the audience.

Title and history of *Twelfth Night*

'Twelfth Night' is the name given to the night preceding the Christian feast of the Epiphany which occurs on January 6th. Formerly, Christmas celebrations lasted for twelve days and ended on a note of great joy and merriment. It has been suggested that the Christian 'Twelfth Night' replaced an earlier pagan ritual associated with changes in the natural order. It was the time of the year when coldness was about to be replaced by warmth, darkness by light and so the revels associated with the festival involved the reversal of roles.

There is not much in Shakespeare's play that relates directly to this festival though some unusual occurrences do take place. Viola disguises herself as a man and is then wooed by another woman, and Sebastian, who was thought to be dead, is shown to be alive. Shakespeare's choice of title was probably intended to draw attention to the spirit of joy that permeates much of the play, but his alternative title *What You Will* suggests two interpretations, firstly that the title is not very important and so one may call it whatever one wishes, or, secondly, it may be a comment on the non-realistic quality of the play in which many wishes are fulfilled. In 1623 the play was referred to as *Malvolio* possibly because his character is among the most interesting in the play and also because he takes part in many of the most amusing scenes.

Twelfth Night does not appear in the 1598 list of Shakespeare's plays but was referred to by John Manningham in 1602 and so it seems likely that it was composed between these dates. There is additional evidence to suggest that it was presented on Twelfth Night 1601 at Whitehall in the presence of Queen Elizabeth and her guest of honour, an Italian nobleman called Virginio Orsino. It even seems likely that Shakespeare named the Duke in his play 'Orsino' as a compliment to the Queen's guest.

The story of twins being so alike that no one can tell them apart goes back to Plautus but tales involving a girl disguised as a page-boy serving the man she loved were so common in the sixteenth century that it is impossible to decide exactly which sources Shakespeare used for his plot. It seems likely, however, that he knew an Italian comedy *Gl'Ingan-*

nati, that is, *The Deceived Ones*, which had a theme similar to that of *Twelfth Night* and an English version of the same story published by Barnabe Riche in 1581, though it should be added that Shakespeare's play is not identical in character or treatment with either.

A note on the text

Twelfth Night was first printed in the Folio of 1623. Its text was very clear and most of the obvious misprints were corrected in the second Folio of 1632. All subsequent editions have been based on these Folios though the majority of recent printings have modernised the spelling and regularised the punctuation. The main difference between modern editions is in the numbering of lines. The acts and scenes are the same but the numbering of prose lines differs depending on the size of the print and width of the page. Since more than half of the play is written in prose, the line numbers can differ considerably. The Arden Edition* of *Twelfth Night* has been used for all quotations in these notes, but if the student uses a different text it should not be difficult to find the quoted lines in his own edition.

---

*See Part 5: Suggestions for further reading.

Part 2

Summaries
of TWELFTH NIGHT

A general summary

Viola and her twin brother Sebastian are so alike that people cannot tell them apart. On a sea journey they are shipwrecked off the coast of Illyria. They are separated from each other and, although they are rescued, they both believe the other has been drowned. Viola disguises herself as a young man and, under the assumed name of Cesario, she finds employment with Orsino, Duke of Illyria. Soon, she is in love with the Duke although he is infatuated with Countess Olivia. Orsino sends 'Cesario' to plead with Olivia on his behalf. Olivia refuses to consider Orsino's proposal but finds herself deeply attracted to 'Cesario'.

Olivia's steward, Malvolio, antagonises many members of her household by his arrogant self-righteousness and by his attempts to end the revels of Olivia's kinsman, Sir Toby Belch, and his gullible acquaintance, Sir Andrew Aguecheek. Sir Andrew has been persuaded that Olivia will eventually agree to marry him and, while he waits in hope, he spends his money in carousing with Sir Toby. Maria, one of Olivia's gentlewomen, allies with Sir Toby to bring about Malvolio's downfall. They trick him into believing that Olivia is in love with him. His subsequent behaviour convinces Olivia that he is mad and she agrees that he should be locked up.

Sir Andrew sees how affectionately Olivia treats 'Cesario' and he is encouraged by Sir Toby to challenge this rival in love to a duel. Sir Andrew is a coward and 'Cesario', as a woman, clearly does not want to fight. Sir Toby, however, feels that such a duel would be amusing and so he determines that it should take place. He tells them separately that the other is a superb swordsman and so, terrified, they face each other in a duel.

In the meantime, Sebastian has arrived in the city with his friend Antonio who rescued him from the sea. Antonio had previously fought against Duke Orsino and so he does not want to be seen by any of Orsino's men. For this reason he and Sebastian separate when they reach the city. Antonio comes upon Sir Andrew and 'Cesario' duelling and immediately goes to 'Cesario's' defence thinking that 'Cesario' is Sebastian. When 'Cesario' thanks Antonio as if he were a stranger Antonio is most upset because he cannot understand why his friend refuses to acknowledge him. Before explanations can be given Antonio is arrested for his old crime.

While Sebastian wanders around the city he meets Sir Andrew and Sir Toby who think he is 'Cesario'. Sir Andrew decides to continue the duel and strikes Sebastian. Sebastian defends himself well and soon overcomes Sir Andrew. Sir Toby then challenges Sebastian but their duel is stopped by the arrival of Olivia. She also thinks Sebastian is 'Cesario' and she repeats her love for him. Sebastian is bewildered but since he finds Olivia very beautiful he agrees to marry her.

Eventually, 'Cesario' and Sebastian meet and all the problems arising from mistaken identity are solved. Olivia keeps her marriage vows to Sebastian, Malvolio is released from his confinement, Sir Toby marries Maria and the Duke realises he loves Viola. The play ends, as it began, with music.

Detailed summaries

Act I Scene 1

Scene 1 begins to establish the setting of the play. Orsino, Duke of Illyria (an imaginary Mediterranean country) is in love with Countess Olivia, but she does not return his feeling. This scene reveals some of the Duke's characteristics. He appears moody, sentimental and fond of music.

NOTES AND GLOSSARY:

Duke: Orsino is called 'Duke' in all stage directions. In the text of the play, however, he is referred to as 'Duke' four times and as 'Count' seventeen times. It would appear, therefore, that in this play Shakespeare uses the titles interchangeably

That instant was I turn'd into a hart: Shakespeare puns on the similarity of sound of 'hart' and 'heart'. The Duke implies that as soon as he saw Olivia his love became the dominant passion of his life and also that she treated him as cruelly as a pack of hounds treats a deer

when liver, brain, and heart . . .: according to Elizabethan belief, the liver was the source of the passions, the brain the source of intelligent thought and the heart the source of the emotions. The fact that there is considerable overlap between the passions and the emotions has resulted in the heart's now being regarded as the seat of both passions and emotions

Eye-offending brine: tears
the rich golden shaft: Cupid's golden arrows caused one to love whereas his leaden arrows caused one to dislike the first person seen after being struck by an arrow

---

Act I Scene 2

The action now shifts to the coast of Illyria. Viola has been shipwrecked with the captain and a group of sailors. She believes that her twin brother, Sebastian, has been drowned although the captain holds out a hope that Sebastian may have survived. The conversation between Viola and the captain is a means of providing certain information for the audience. We learn that Orsino is unmarried and that Olivia is in mourning for the recent deaths of her father and brother and will not receive the Duke's messengers.

Viola decides to dress as a page and serve the Duke. The captain agrees to keep her secret.

NOTES AND GLOSSARY:
Elysium: this is another word for Heaven
Arion: a Greek poet and musician. His music so charmed a dolphin that it carried him to safety when he jumped into the sea to escape from captivity
character: appearance
Thou shalt present me as an eunuch to him: Viola suggests that she will seek employment as a 'eunuch'. It may be that the word is used to mean 'one who serves' because her role as eunuch is never again mentioned. When we next meet Viola she has disguised herself as Cesario and become one of the Duke's pages

---

Act I Scene 3

In this scene we are introduced to a third set of characters, a set which is responsible for the humorous sub-plot. Sir Toby Belch (his surname suggests over-indulgence) is a drunkard and a reveller. He is a relation of Olivia and lives in her house. Olivia does not approve of Sir Toby's behaviour and he is informed of this disapproval by Maria, Olivia's gentlewoman companion. Sir Toby has invited a drinking associate, Sir Andrew Aguecheek, to stay in Olivia's house. Sir Andrew has been fooled into spending his money by Sir Toby's assurances that he will eventually win Olivia's love. Sir Andrew's doubts as to the likelihood of an eventual marriage are quelled by Sir Toby. They joke about dancing and merrymaking and determine to enjoy themselves.

NOTES AND GLOSSARY:

your cousin: in the Elizabethan period this was a general term for a relation though not necessarily a close relation. Sir Toby calls Olivia his niece but this term too was less specific than it is now. Sir Toby is an older, male kinsman but the exact relationship between Olivia and Sir Toby is never made clear

Aguecheek: at the time Shakespeare wrote the name 'Aguecheek' would have suggested a man who was extremely thin and also cowardly

Ducats: gold coins

Good Mistress Accost, I desire better acquaintance . . .: much of this passage, as indeed much of the scene, can be interpreted on two levels, as humorous banter and as sexually suggestive dialogue

galliard, back-trick, coranto: the names of several dance steps occur in this scene. A 'galliard' was a fast dance, a 'back-trick' was a backward step in a dance and a 'coranto' was a quick, running movement

under the star of a galliard . . .: the reference to the stars and constellations underlines the Elizabethan belief that human events were influenced by heavenly bodies

---

Act I Scene 4

Scene 4 takes place in the Duke's household. Within three days of her arrival at his palace, Viola in the guise of a page, Cesario, has won the Duke's affection and has been entrusted to carry his message of love to Olivia. Viola would prefer not to be such a messenger because she has fallen in love with the Duke herself. Nevertheless, she agrees to do his bidding:

> I'll do my best
> To woo your lady: yet, a barful strife!
> Who'er I woo, myself would be his wife.
>   (lines 40–2)

One of the themes of *Twelfth Night* is falling in love at first sight. This is the first example in the play, but others are soon to follow.

NOTES AND GLOSSARY:

address your gait: direct your steps

leap all civil bounds: the Duke advises his 'page' to overlook the limits of normal courtesy

nuncio: messenger

pipe:	a small, high-pitched voice
thy constellation:	the Duke's reference to Viola's 'constellation' implies that her behaviour and disposition were conditioned by the heavenly bodies
barful strife:	very hard to achieve

Act I Scene 5

In this long scene we first meet Olivia and her serious, self-righteous steward, Malvolio, whose name implies 'bad will'. They join Maria and the Clown who are engaged in a verbal battle of the type that is often found in Elizabethan drama. Because of her self-imposed seven-year period of mourning Olivia has little time for clowns but she is less critical of them than Malvolio is. He is even critical of Olivia for arguing with the Clown, but Olivia tells him he is at fault:

> O, you are sick of self-love, Malvolio, and taste
> with a distempered appetite.
> (lines 89–90)

Maria, who left the stage on the arrival of Olivia and Malvolio, returns to say that a young man (that is, Viola disguised as Cesario) wishes to speak to her. Olivia suspects 'he' is from Orsino and tells Maria to send 'him' away.

Sir Toby comes in, half drunk as usual, and is criticised by Olivia for his debauched behaviour.

Malvolio returns with the message that the young 'man' refuses to go away without seeing Olivia. Eventually, Olivia agrees to admit 'him'.

Viola in her role as Cesario the page attempts to speak to Olivia of Duke Orsino's love. In spite of all 'his' efforts, however, Olivia refuses to reconsider her attitude to the Duke. She is deeply impressed by the youth and beauty of the page and tells 'him' to come again. Olivia offers 'him' money which 'he' refuses:

> I am no fee'd post, lady; keep your purse;
> My master, not myself, lacks recompense
> (lines 288–9)

thus implying that 'he' is not just a messenger who takes bribes and that it is the Duke rather than 'himself' who lacks his reward.

When the page leaves, Olivia realises that she has fallen in love. She sends Malvolio after 'him' with a ring which she pretends 'he' left behind and invites 'him' to return the following day.

By the end of Act I we thus have a complex situation where Olivia loves Viola in her guise as a page, where Viola loves Orsino but cannot tell him so because of her disguise and where Orsino loves Olivia.

NOTES AND GLOSSARY:

Quinapalus: an invented authority. The Clown wishes to make his statement sound authoritative and so he creates a Latin-sounding name

cucullus non facit monachum: (*Latin*) this proverb means 'the hood does not make the monk' and implies that one should not judge by externals

mouse: a frequent Elizabethan endearment. Compare its use here with Sir Andrew's description of Maria as 'fair shrew' (I.3.46) where 'shrew' may mean both 'mouse' and 'bad-tempered woman'

I am no fox: the fox symbolises 'cunning'

Bird-bolts: flat-headed arrows used for shooting birds. The implication of Olivia's statement is that a person who is 'generous, guiltless, and of free disposition' tends to underestimate dangerous situations

Now Mercury endue thee with leasing: Mercury was the god of lying and deceit. The word 'leasing' which also occurs in this line meant 'lying'. It is no longer used with this meaning in modern English

Pia mater: Latin equivalent of 'gentle mother'. The term was used to mean 'brain'

I am not that I play: I am not what I appear to be. This is an example of dramatic irony. The audience knows that Cesario is really Viola and so, clearly, not the young man she appears to be

'tis not that time of moon with me: the phases of the moon were associated with irrational behaviour and so Olivia is implying that she is not in the mood to listen to a wildly extravagant speech

I hold the olive in my hand: the olive branch symbolises 'peace'

Make me a willow cabin: the willow symbolises 'grief, sadness'

The County's man: Shakespeare often uses 'County' for 'Count'. In the same line Olivia says: 'he left this ring behind him'. It would appear that she offered this excuse to Malvolio to prevent him suspecting her feeling for Cesario and also to give herself an excuse for inviting 'him' back the following day

---

Act II Scene 1

This scene reveals that Viola's twin brother, Sebastian, has been rescued from the shipwreck by Antonio, a sea captain. Antonio has become very fond of Sebastian and tries to dissuade him from going to the main city of Illyria, partly because he, Antonio, has been in trouble with the Illyrian authorities. Sebastian feels he must visit the city. He believes that Viola has been drowned and stresses the similarity in their appearances, thus preparing the audience for the mistakes in identity which occur. Antonio, in spite of the danger, decides to accompany Sebastian to Orsino's court.

NOTES AND GLOSSARY:

nor will you not that I go with you: in Elizabethan English a double negative could be used for emphasis in a way that is no longer possible in the standard language

distemper: means here to contaminate, infect. Sebastian urges Antonio not to accompany him in case the bad luck with which Sebastian has been touched should spread to Antonio

my determinate voyage is mere extravagancy: I am determined to make this journey even though it will serve no purpose

my name is Sebastian: to the reader these lines may seem unnecessary but they serve the purpose of explaining Sebastian's identity and background to the audience

Messaline: like Illyria, an imaginary place

born in an hour: the phrase means 'born within an hour of each other' and emphasises once again the fact that Viola and Sebastian are twins

If you will not murder me for my love: Antonio has become so fond of Sebastian that he suggests he would die of grief if he were not permitted to accompany Sebastian

---

Act II Scene 2

In Act I, Scene 5 Olivia had sent Malvolio after Cesario (Viola) with a ring. She pretended the ring had been left behind by Cesario but, in reality, it is a token of her love for the young 'page'. Viola realises that Olivia has fallen in love with her and feels sorry because such love cannot be satisfied:

> She loves me, sure: . . .
> Poor lady, she were better love a dream.
> (lines 21 and 25)

She also feels a little sorry for the complicated situation in which she finds herself. As a woman she loves Orsino, but Orsino loves Olivia and Olivia has now fallen in love with Viola in her guise as Cesario, the Duke's page. Nevertheless, she decides that, in time, a solution will be found:

O time, thou must untangle this, not I,
It is too hard a knot for me t'untie.
       (lines 39–40)

NOTES AND GLOSSARY:

She took the ring of me: Viola does not wish to embarrass Olivia in front of Malvolio and so she pretends she *did* give a ring to Olivia

pregnant enemy: the 'enemy who is always ready to take advantage of one' and is a euphemism for the devil. Viola is really lamenting the fact that her disguise is a form of deception and has already caused several problems

---

Act II Scene 3

Sir Toby and Sir Andrew are, once again, the focus of attention. They are celebrating late the same night in Olivia's house and they have been joined by Maria and the Clown. Maria warns them that Olivia has been disturbed by their revelry and is sending Malvolio to throw them out. Malvolio reminds them of the time and insists that they must either stop their noisy celebration or leave Olivia's house. Malvolio is mocked by Sir Toby and the Clown but, before leaving them, Malvolio reminds Maria that she will lose Olivia's favour if she continues her association with the revellers.

When he has gone, Sir Andrew suggests that he will challenge Malvolio to a duel and then annoy him by not turning up. Maria assures them that she has a better idea for making a fool of Malvolio. She can write like Olivia and her plan is to make him find some letters which will convince him that Olivia loves him. Maria believes that he is such a 'Puritan' (line 146), that is, serious and straitlaced, that he will believe the contents of the letters and in this way she and the others will be able to make a fool of Malvolio.

NOTES AND GLOSSARY:

diluculo surgere saluberrimum est: this Latin proverb means 'it is very healthy to rise early'

the four elements: everything in the world was thought to be composed of the four elements—fire, air, water and earth

stoup: a large vessel which held liquids

the picture of 'we three': a common Elizabethan inn sign involved a picture of two fools, and the caption 'we three' which appeared under the sign suggested that the onlooker was also a fool

the fool has an excellent breast: Sir Andrew implies that the Clown has an excellent singing voice

thou spok'st of Pigrogromitus . . .: the names Pigrogromitus, Vapians and Queubus are invented names and serve the same purpose as Quinapalus (I.5.33), in that they sound authoritative

leman: sweetheart, beloved. The word is no longer current in standard English

I did impeticos thy gratillity . . .: the Clown is deliberately playing with language, thanking Sir Andrew for his money, insulting Malvolio's long nose, praising Olivia's white hand and suggesting that law-officers (that is, Myrmidons) are not found in places where alcohol is drunk

testril: a small coin

A contagious breath: Sir Toby deliberately encourages Sir Andrew to use an inappropriate word because 'contagious' means 'catching a disease by contact' and is generally applied to an illness

But shall we make the welkin dance indeed?: But shall we make the sky dance or at least appear to dance by getting drunk? Sir Toby suggests that they combine to sing a three-part song (that is, a catch). The reference to 'weavers' is based on the belief that weavers often sang psalms. This was partly true because many Elizabethan weavers were Calvinist refugees from Holland

I am a dog at a catch: I am good at singing

My lady's a Cataian: by this time Sir Toby is drunk and so does not respond sensibly to Maria's warning that Malvolio will hear them and put them out. He reproaches Olivia calling her a 'Cataian', that is, a person from Cathay/China, refers to himself and his friends as being 'politicians', that is, well able to look after their own interests, and calls Malvolio by the name of a popular dance tune 'Peg-a-Ramsey'. In any case, he believes that his relationship with Olivia will be his safeguard

Sneck up!: this is roughly equivalent to: 'Be hanged!' or 'Be damned!'

Cakes and ale: these were associated with festivals and merrymaking and so were disliked by Puritans. Sir Toby implies that merrymaking will continue in spite of people like Malvolio

rub your chain with crumbs: one method of cleaning a chain was to rub it with breadcrumbs. Sir Toby was implying that Malvolio was over-zealous in the performance of his duty as steward

The devil a Puritan that he is: Malvolio is condemned as a 'kind of Puritan'. The word was sometimes used as a synonym for 'spoilsport'. Maria's criticisms of Malvolio, that he was a time-server, an ass, and a hypocrite, need not be taken too seriously. Malvolio (line 120–3) had just warned her that her association with Sir Toby might cause her to lose Olivia's favour. It is worth remembering that Olivia thought very highly of him. When she thinks he is ill, she says: 'I would not have him miscarry (that is come to harm) for the half of my dowry.' (III.4.63–4)

Penthesilea: a Queen of the Amazons. Sir Toby is complimenting Maria for the excellence of her scheme to trick Malvolio

sack: a type of sherry. Sir Toby suggests that they 'burn some sack' meaning that they should warm some sherry

---

Act II Scene 4

Once again we are in the Duke's palace and once again the Duke is listening to music and discussing the suffering endured by lovers. To his surprise, Cesario (Viola) speaks feelingly about love and explains that 'he' loves one who looks like the Duke and is about the Duke's age. The audience is, of course, aware that Viola loves the Duke. They discuss the constancy of men and women in love and Feste, the Clown, echoes their remarks by singing about unrequited love. When Feste has gone out, the Duke once again sends Cesario to Olivia to say that Orsino loves her for herself alone and not for her possessions and that such love should no longer be refused.

NOTES AND GLOSSARY:

motions: emotions

favour: here 'favour' means 'face' whereas the phrase 'by your favour' in line 25 is the equivalent of 'by your leave' or 'if it pleases you/please'

Let still the woman take an elder than herself: the Duke implies that a woman should marry an older man. In this way, she will be young enough to adapt to his ways

spinster: a woman who spins

let thy love be younger than thyself: the Duke continues to give advice, urging that a man should choose a woman younger than himself or else his affection will not last

Bones: bone bobbins used in the making of lace

in sad cypress let me be laid: this line from the Clown's song means: 'Let me be laid in a coffin made of cypress wood'. The cypress, like the willow tree, symbolised sadness and mourning

a very opal: an opal is a jewel which changes colour in different lights. In this it resembles the 'changeable taffeta' of line 74

That suffers surfeit, cloyment: both surfeit and cloyment refer to the feeling of over-satisfaction. If one longs for a special type of food and then eats too much of it, one grows tired of it and longs for something else

bide no denay: accept no refusal. The old form denay for 'denial' is used for the rhyme

---

Act II Scene 5

This scene enacts the tricking of Malvolio by Maria, Sir Toby, Sir Andrew and Fabian who is a member of Olivia's household staff. Maria tells them to hide in the garden near the spot where Malvolio will pass and she drops a letter on the path. Malvolio picks up the letter, opens it and believes it was written by Olivia to her 'unknown beloved'. The writer has written:

I may command where I adore;
But silence, like a Lucrece knife,
With bloodless stroke my heart doth gore;
M.O.A.I. doth sway my life.
(lines 106–9)

To the delight of Sir Toby and his friends, Malvolio immediately believes that the letter was meant for him. After all, Olivia can command him. He is her steward, and the letters M, O, A and I all occur in his name, though in a different order. The remainder of the letter instructs the 'beloved' to be firm with Sir Toby and with the servants, to dress more fashionably in yellow stockings and to smile more frequently.

Malvolio takes the letter seriously and decides to follow its instructions. He believes that one can be great because of one's birth, one's achievements or because of circumstances:

Some are born great, some achieve greatness, and some have greatness thrust upon 'em.
(lines 145–6)

He is to be great according to the third category and so he goes off intent on becoming Olivia's husband: 'I will do everything that thou wilt have me' (line 179). Shakespeare's audience would have noticed that Malvolio is already using the intimate pronoun 'thou' when referring to Olivia.

Sir Toby and the others are delighted with the success of their trick. Indeed, Maria's ingenuity pleases Sir Toby so much that he claims he would be prepared to marry her even without a dowry. Maria tells them to expect further amusement because, if Malvolio follows the instructions in the letter, he will undoubtedly offend Olivia, who may then feel obliged to dismiss him.

NOTES AND GLOSSARY:

if I lose a scruple of this sport: Fabian does not want to lose a 'scruple', or the 'smallest part' of the entertainment that will result from making a fool of Malvolio

sheep-biter: a derogatory term applied to Malvolio. It may be a reference to his Puritanism. Puritans attacked the excesses of other Christians even though as Christians they were 'sheep' of the same 'flock'

bear baiting: popular Elizabethan sport in which bears were goaded to make them more ferocious. Puritans disapproved of such savage pastimes

my metal of India: Sir Toby addresses Maria as 'my metal of India' implying that she is very precious, like Indian gold

she did affect me: she admired and had some affection for me

The Lady of the Strachy married the yeoman: Malvolio finds an example of a lady marrying a man of lower rank

O for a stone-bow: Sir Toby's 'stone-bow' was either a cross-bow which fired stones or a catapult

cars: chariots

the impressure her Lucrece: the imprint of her ring. The nobility used their rings to put an impression on the wax with which they sealed letters. Ladies frequently had seal-rings with the image of the much-admired Roman Lucretia on them. Lucretia stabbed herself after being raped

brock: badger. Badgers were supposed to give off a very bad smell.

Fustian: bombastic. Fabian implies that the riddle is well suited to Malvolio

stallien: a type of hawk. Expressions derived from hunting and hawking were very popular at the time of Shakespeare

Sowter: a hound

Sowter will cry upon't . . .: Fabian suggests that Malvolio will follow the scent even though anyone else would realise it was false

let thy blood and spirit: let your courage. Both words are synonyms for 'courage'

thy yellow stockings: the clothes—'yellow stockings' and 'cross-garters' —would not have been worn by conscientious Puritans. They were selected by Maria to make Malvolio conspicuous and to annoy Olivia

I will be point-device the very man: I shall dress and behave exactly the way the letter suggests I should

habits: clothing

the Sophy: the Shah of Persia. In Elizabethan times, the Shah was regarded as having extraordinary wealth

aqua-vitae: (*Latin*) water of life. The term was applied to brandy

Tartar: the word 'Tartarus' was also used for 'hell'

Act III Scene 1

The setting is again Olivia's garden, though this time Viola, in her guise as Cesario, has come to plead Orsino's case to Olivia. Cesario talks to Feste, the Clown, while 'he' waits and they indulge in the verbal games so characteristic of the Elizabethan theatre. Feste is given a coin in return for the pleasure his wit has given to Cesario. In return, Feste wishes that Cesario may soon have a beard. 'He' replies: 'I am almost sick for one' (lines 47–8), but, by this, she implies that she is almost sick because of her longing for the Duke.

Sir Toby and Sir Andrew join Cesario but they are asked to leave when Olivia appears. Olivia can no longer contain her passion:

> Cesario, by the roses of the spring,
> By maidhood, honour, truth, and everything,
> I love thee so . . .
>   (lines 151–3)

Cesario cannot accept Olivia's love and yet cannot reveal the reason why without admitting 'his' disguise. Olivia thinks Cesario is unfeeling and cruel and yet cannot bear the thought of not seeing 'him' again. She tells Cesario to return to her in the slight hope that she might be persuaded by 'him' to love Orsino.

NOTES AND GLOSSARY:
chev'ril: also spelt cheveril. This is a young goat or kid. Its hide was used for making gloves

dost thou live by the Tabor: there is a pun on the phrase 'live by'. Viola intends to ask the Clown if he makes his living by playing the drum. He chooses to interpret it to mean 'live close to' and so answers that he lives near the church

I'll no more with thee: Viola tells the Clown that if he insists on playing word-games she will not continue the conversation. The Clown does not displease her, however, as is clear from the fact that she gives him a tip

I would play Lord Pandarus of Phrygia . . .: the story of Pandarus, Troilus and Cressida was well known in England and Shakespeare subsequently wrote a play called *Troilus and Cressida*. Troilus loved Cressida and was helped by her uncle Pandarus to win her. Cressida vowed her love for Troilus but proved faithless and eventually became a leper and a beggar

welkin: normally sky, but here the Clown implies that Viola's identity is beyond his knowledge

Dieu vous garde . . .: Sir Andrew uses a courteous French greeting meaning: 'May God preserve you, sir' to which Viola replies: 'And you too: At your service' (literally, your servant)

list: objective. Viola, as Cesario, is going to see Olivia

taste: try. Sir Toby says 'Walk. Put your legs to the test'

prevent: come before, anticipate

to your own most pregnant and vouchsafed ear: Viola insists that what she has to say is for Olivia's ears only. In the context, 'pregnant' means 'receptive' and 'vouchsafed' means 'granted'

music from the spheres: this is a reference to the belief that the movement of the stars and planets produced music which could not be heard by human ears. (see p.6)

cypress: here the word is used to mean a piece of fine, gauze-like material

degree to: a step in the direction of

grize: small step

'Tis a vulgar proof: it is a common human experience

Westward-ho: this was a call used by boatmen on the Thames to indicate they were about to go towards Westminster

Act III Scene 2

Sir Andrew has seen Olivia's love for Cesario and so determines to leave her household and give up his attempt to win her in marriage.

Fabian and Sir Toby wish to keep him there as long as his money lasts and so they suggest that Olivia secretly loves Sir Andrew and wants to make him jealous by *appearing* to lavish her affection on Cesario.

Sir Andrew, like Malvolio,is easily tricked into believing what he wants to believe. Sir Toby suggests that the best way to win Olivia's heart would be to challenge Cesario to a duel. Sir Andrew agrees and goes off to write his challenge. Since Sir Toby and Fabian are only interested in Sir Andrew because of his money they are not disturbed by the prospect of his fighting a duel. Indeed, they feel sure that it will provide them with some extra amusement.

At this point Maria comes in and explains that Malvolio has been absolutely fooled by the letter he found. He has dressed himself up as the letter suggested he should and is smiling continuously. Maria believes that his smiling will so infuriate Olivia that she may well strike him. They all leave to see what will happen between Olivia and Malvolio.

NOTES AND GLOSSARY:

Thy reason dear venom: Sir Toby's remark including 'dear venom' which literally means 'dear poison' must be interpreted in the sense of: 'Give us your reasons for this terrible decision'

orchard: garden

The double gilt of opportunity: Fabian is claiming that Sir Andrew has an excellent opportunity. A 'golden opportunity' is one not to be missed and Sir Andrew's is doubly golden

I had as lief be a Brownist: I'd rather be a Brownist. Robert Brown who lived from about 1550 to 1633 founded a Puritan sect whose members were called 'Brownists'. This is a further example of Sir Andrew's dislike of Puritans

write it in a martial hand, be curst and brief: Sir Toby advises Sir Andrew to write a letter which is fierce and to the point

if thou thou'st him: the use of 'thou' in the letter of challenge is an intentional insult to the recipient

the bed of Ware: this enormous bed, over three metres square, is now in the Victoria and Albert Museum in London

This is a dear manikin to you: Fabian suggests that Sir Toby has enjoyed treating Sir Andrew as his puppet. Sir Toby agrees and adds that he has persuaded Sir Andrew to spend a great deal of money

the youngest wren of nine: Sir Toby affectionately refers to Maria's short stature by calling her 'the youngest wren of nine', that is 'the last and the smallest of the brood'

cubiculo: a little room. Here presumably, it means a bedroom

if you desire the spleen: if you want a really good laugh

renegado: this term was applied to a Christian who abandoned his religion

can believe such impossible passages of grossness: Maria implies that they will not be able to believe what they see

like a pedant that keeps a school i' the church: like an old-fashioned schoolmaster

the new map: the map referred to was probably the one printed in 1599. It included more detailed information of other parts of the world than earlier maps

---

Act III Scene 3

Sebastian and Antonio have now reached the city. Sebastian is eager to see all he can but Antonio has to be careful because if he is recognised he would be in trouble with the authorities. Once, in the past, he had fought a sea-battle against Duke Orsino's ships. Antonio therefore decides to see to the lodgings and he gives Sebastian his purse in case the young man needs money. They arrange to meet later at an inn, called the Elephant, which is in a quiet area of the town, and then they set off in different directions.

NOTES AND GLOSSARY:

jealousy: anxiety, apprehension

skilless: lacking in skill or knowledge. Antonio is commenting on Sebastian's ignorance of the country

uncurrent pay: counterfeit or worthless money. Sebastian is suggesting that the mere saying of 'thanks' is a poor return for kindness

relics: not 'ruins' as in our modern usage, but the 'famous buildings of the city'

the Count his galleys: the Count's ships. The phrase illustrates a common Elizabethan possessive construction

here's my purse: Antonio gives his purse to Sebastian saying that Sebastian may see something which he would like to buy, but without Antonio's purse he would not have enough money

---

Act III Scene 4

Olivia has again sent for Cesario and is anxious about how to behave when 'he' arrives. She feels in need of some solemn advice and sends for Malvolio. Maria tells Olivia that Malvolio is acting strangely and so must have gone mad. Nevertheless, Olivia wants to see him and is very disturbed by the changes she sees in his appearance and behaviour. Malvolio quotes from the letter he believes Olivia wrote but, since she knows nothing about the letter, she is perplexed. When Cesario is announced Olivia asks Maria to have Malvolio well looked after because she treasures him:

> Good Maria, let this fellow be looked to. Where's my cousin Toby?
> Let some of my people have a special care of him; I would not have
> him miscarry for the half of my dowry.
>   (lines 59–63)

Malvolio is pleased by this reference and behaves very insolently to Sir Toby, Maria and Fabian. They try to restrain Malvolio suggesting he is mad. Malvolio, however, gets away from them but Sir Toby and Maria determine that he must be locked away. (It was fairly typical Elizabethan behaviour to lock up people who were thought to be insane.) Sir Andrew comes in with his written challenge and Sir Toby urges him to wait for Cesario at the street corner. In the meantime, Sir Toby decides to deliver Sir Andrew's challenge verbally because, if Cesario saw the written challenge, 'he' would know what a coward Sir Andrew was. Sir Toby plans to tell Cesario that Sir Andrew is a fierce warrior.

Meanwhile, Olivia and Cesario continue their discussion about love. Olivia thinks Cesario is very cold but the audience knows that Cesario is in no position to return Olivia's love. Olivia, in spite of Cesario's lack of love, urges 'him' to come and see her again. Before Cesario can return to the Duke's court Sir Toby offers Sir Andrew's challenge. Cesario is terrified at the very idea of a duel especially with one whom Sir Toby describes as 'quick, skilful, and deadly' but rather than reveal that 'he' is a woman in disguise the duel is accepted. Sir Toby succeeds in persuading both Sir Andrew and Cesario that their opponent is virtually unbeatable. Neither really wants to fight but neither is allowed to back down.

The duel begins but almost as soon as they have crossed swords Antonio comes on the scene. He mistakes Cesario for Sebastian and goes to 'his' defence. Sir Toby is annoyed that the humorous duel between Cesario and Sir Andrew has been interrupted so he too joins the fight and is wounded by Antonio. The officers of the guard put an end to the fighting, recognise Antonio and put him under arrest for his old crime against Duke Orsino. Antonio, still believing that Cesario is Sebastian, asks Cesario for his purse because he will need money for his defence. Cesario does not know what he is talking about but offers half of 'his' own money to Antonio. Antonio is amazed at Sebastian's ingratitude and is dragged away by the officers.

Left alone, Viola begins to put the pieces of the puzzle together.

She has been mistaken for a man called Sebastian, a man rescued from the sea by Antonio, so she now has hope that her twin brother was not drowned after all.

Sir Toby is angry with Cesario because he (Sir Toby) was wounded in the fight, but also because Cesario appeared to deny 'his' friend, Antonio. He tells Sir Andrew that Cesario is a coward after all and, hearing this, Sir Andrew decides to follow 'him' and continue the duel.

NOTES AND GLOSSARY:

He is sure possessed: Maria suggests that Malvolio is 'possessed' by the devil. In this way she prepares Olivia for Malvolio's strange appearance and behaviour

the sweet Roman hand: Malvolio is complimenting Olivia on her hand-writing but, since Olivia did not write the letter, she does not understand his reference

nightingales answer daws: Malvolio is probably being scornful. His answer is the equivalent of: 'Should a nightingale (that is a bird of beauty) answer a jackdaw (that is one of the commonest birds in England)?'

midsummer madness: the midsummer moon was thought to induce mad-ness. Olivia is so surprised by the encounter with Malvolio that she assumes he must be temporarily insane

let this fellow be looked to: Olivia's command that Malvolio should be cared for shows that she values her steward highly

miscarry: come to any harm

I have limed her: I have caught her. Birds were often caught by spreading lime on the ground. The word 'lime' thus took on the meaning of 'catch'. Malvolio suggests that he has caught Olivia

after my degree: according to my rank and status

Legion himself possessed him: Sir Toby suggests that Malvolio is pos-sessed not by one devil but by innumerable devils. He is referring to the account in Chapter V of St Mark's Gospel where Jesus cast out a legion of devils from a man who was possessed

bawcock: handsome, fine fellow. Sir Toby is teasing Malvolio

'tis not for gravity to play at cherry-pit with Satan . . .: Sir Toby pretends that he believes Malvolio is possessed and tells Malvolio that it is wrong to be on good terms with the devil because the devil is covered with evil in the same way as a coalminer is covered with coal dust

minx: a brazen, impudent woman. Malvolio's reference to Maria as a 'minx' is a calculated insult

genius: the word is applied to Malvolio's 'soul' and not to his 'intelligence'

pursue him now, lest the device take air: Maria suggests that they should lock Malvolio up, implying that if he were free his madness might grow worse

we'll have him in a dark room . . .: the treatment of madmen in Elizabethan England often involved their being locked in a dark room. Since Olivia believes that Malvolio is mad, Sir Toby and his friends will be able to lock him up until they decide to be merciful and release him

for a May morning: May was often associated with holidays and games. When Fabian sees Sir Andrew he suggests that they will be able to have more fun by making a fool of Sir Andrew

bumbailey: a bailiff who tried to arrest a suspect by sneaking up behind him

now will not I deliver his letter: Sir Toby decides to deliver the challenge verbally since the letter is so badly composed that Cesario would immediately realise Sir Andrew was a fool

clodpole: fool, blockhead

Cockatrices: mythical serpents, also called 'basilisks'. It was thought they could kill their prey simply by looking at it

strip your sword: Sir Toby instructs Viola to draw out 'his' sword immediately and be prepared to face a terrifying adversary

even to a mortal: Fabian frightens Viola by suggesting that Sir Andrew will fight to the death

virago: or less frequently, a firago, a female warrior. It is ironic that Sir Toby applies the term to Viola without realising that she is a woman

fencer to the Sophy: this is the second reference in the play to the Sophy, the Shah of Persia (see also II.5.181)

undertaker: meddler, someone who 'undertakes' to deal with matters which do not concern him

there's half my coffer: Viola offers to give Antonio half of the money in her possession

In nature, there's no blemish . . .: Antonio sums up his disillusionment by saying that Sebastian was perfect on the outside but worthless within, like a well-made but empty container

Act IV Scene 1

Olivia sends Feste, the Clown, after Cesario but Feste meets Sebastian instead. Sebastian is completely perplexed by Feste who, clearly, mistakes him for someone else. To add to his confusion, Sir Toby and Sir Andrew appear and Sir Andrew strikes Sebastian. Sebastian fights back, soon defeats Sir Andrew and is then attacked by Sir Toby. The Clown goes to tell Olivia what is happening and she hastens to rescue her beloved Cesario. She sends Sir Toby away, asks Sebastian's forgiveness: 'Be not offended, dear Cesario' (line 49), and invites him back to her house. Sebastian does not understand what is happening but he agrees to go with the beautiful Olivia.

NOTES AND GLOSSARY:

Will you make me believe that I am not sent for you?: the Clown has been sent to find Cesario but he believes that Sebastian is Cesario

I am afraid this great lubber the world will prove a cockney: the Clown suggests that everyone is behaving strangely. A 'cockney' was a 'small egg'

foolish Greek: foolish jester

I'll have an action of battery against him: since Sir Andrew cannot beat Sebastian in a duel he claims that he will sue him in court for assault

rudesby: ruffian

extent: assault

Go with me to my house: Olivia invites Sebastian to go home with her and listen to the many plots Sir Toby has hatched. There is dramatic irony in the fact that Olivia does not know about how Sir Toby has plotted against Malvolio

Or I am mad, or else this is a dream: Sebastian cannot decide whether he is dreaming or whether everyone else is mad. Nevertheless, in spite of not understanding what is happening, he agrees to go home with Olivia

Act IV Scene 2

Malvolio has been locked up in a dark room and is being teased by Maria, Feste and Sir Toby. Feste dresses up as a clergyman, Sir Topas, and goes into the darkened room to discuss religious matters with Malvolio. At first Malvolio is pleased to hear a voice, thinking that he will soon be released but soon he is confused by the nonsense spoken by 'Sir Topas' in his parody of ecclesiastical language. 'Sir Topas' says that he wants to test Malvolio's sanity and asks Malvolio to explain Pythagoras' doctrine of the transmigration of the soul. Malvolio does so and is told that he must accept this non-Christian doctrine. (Pythagoras, a Greek philosopher, had suggested that the soul of a dying person may continue to live in the body of an animal or bird.) Malvolio refuses to change his religious beliefs.

At this stage, Sir Toby feels that the joke has gone too far and wishes they could put an end to it. He is worried about Olivia's reaction when she discovers how they have treated her steward.

Feste returns to Malvolio and after some further teasing agrees to get him some paper and ink so that he might write to Olivia

NOTES AND GLOSSARY:

Sir Topas:	it was not unusual in Elizabethan times to address a priest as 'Sir Priest' or to use his name as is done here and address him as 'Sir Topas'. Shakespeare may also have been punning on the name 'Topas' because the topaz was believed to have the power to cure madness
dissemble:	disguise
competitors:	co-plotters, people involved in the plot to discredit Malvolio
Bonos dies:	this means 'good day' but the Latin is inaccurate

the old hermit of Prague: an invented authority

Gorboduc:	a legendary king of ancient Britain

Why it hath bay windows . . . : Sir Topas uses similes which are intentionally contradictory. Windows are transparent, whereas barricades are opaque. 'Clerestories' are also windows, usually windows in a church

the Egyptians in their fog: the reference here is to one of the plagues of Egypt as recorded in the Bible: Exodus 10, in this case the plague of darkness

thou shalt hold th'opinion of Pythagoras: the Clown in the guise of Sir Topas threatens that he will only certify that Malvolio is sane if Malvolio swears that Pythagoras held valid views on the transmigration of souls

I am for all waters: I am successful at whatever I do

perdie:	this is a corruption of the French *par dieu* meaning 'by God'. Swearing in the name of God was not allowed on the Elizabethan stage and many methods of avoiding direct swearing are apparent in this play.
bibble babble:	idle chatter
God buy you:	God be with you

like to the old vice: Vice was a common character in medieval plays. He often represented such characteristics as Pride, Lust, Greed. In the Middle Ages it had become conventional to show Vice trying to cut the Devil's nails. Hence the reference: 'Pare thy nails, dad' in line 130.

Act IV Scene 3

Sebastian is in Olivia's garden marvelling at his good fortune in being loved by such a beautiful lady. He wishes he could discuss the whole puzzling affair with Antonio but, when he had looked for him at the Elephant inn, Antonio had not been there. (As yet, Sebastian knows nothing of Viola or of Antonio's imprisonment.)

Olivia and a priest join Sebastian in the garden. She asks him to become solemnly betrothed to her in private and promises a public wedding, more suitable to her rank, later on. Sebastian agrees to the betrothal and the scene ends with the three of them going into the chapel.

NOTES AND GLOSSARY:

there he was: he had been there. The use of 'was' is here equivalent to modern 'had been'. In other words, Sebastian had learnt that Antonio had been at the Elephant inn and had gone out to look for Sebastian

chantry: a small chapel in a large house. This one was probably in Olivia's house

whiles: until

they may fairly note this act of mine: Olivia hopes that people will understand and approve of her action when they hear about the secret betrothal

Act V Scene 1

Feste, the Clown, is about to deliver Malvolio's letter to Olivia when Fabian pleads to be allowed to read it. While they are discussing the matter, Duke Orsino arrives with Viola dressed as Cesario and asks Feste to tell Olivia that he has come in person to propose to her. While they are waiting for Olivia to join them, Antonio, still under arrest, comes along. Cesario tells the Duke of Antonio's kindness to 'him'. Duke Orsino recognises Antonio as a brave and honourable enemy and asks him how he came to be arrested. Antonio explains how he had rescued the Duke's page from the sea, had helped him in every way possible, even giving his purse to him, and how his kindness had been repaid by ingratitude.

It is clear that Antonio still believes that Cesario is Sebastian. While the Duke is explaining that Cesario has been in his service for three months and thus could not be the same person who had accompanied Antonio to the city, Olivia comes in. She refuses even to listen to the Duke's protestations of love and is amazed that Cesario, whom she believes to be her betrothed, prepares to leave her and follow the Duke. She asks Cesario where 'he' is going and is told:

> After him I love
> More than I love these eyes, more than my life,
> More, by all mores, than e'er I shall love wife.
> (lines 132–4)

Olivia feels rejected by the man she regards as her husband, so she reveals that they are betrothed and sends for the priest to confirm her story.

Cesario cannot understand what Olivia and the priest are talking about but Orsino believes his page has betrayed his trust and orders Cesario never to come into his presence again. While Cesario is trying to protest 'his' innocence, Sir Andrew and Sir Toby arrive and they claim they have both been wounded by Cesario.

At this point Sebastian appears and everyone can see how similar he and Cesario are in appearance. If it were not for the different colour of their clothes it would be impossible to tell them apart.

Sebastian apologises to Olivia, his 'dear one' for having hurt her kinsman and he greets Antonio affectionately, explaining how worried he had been when he had not found Antonio at their designated meeting place. Then, turning to Cesario, Sebastian asks if they are related. Cesario explains 'his' parentage and how 'he' had thought 'his' brother Sebastian was dead. Sebastian acknowledges the similarity of their stories but is puzzled because he had a sister and not a brother. Cesario admits that 'he' is Viola in disguise.

Sebastian then realises that Olivia had been in love with Viola, but he vows his love for her nonetheless. Duke Orsino shares in the joy of the others because he has become extremely fond of Cesario and now knows that his love is returned. He asks to see Viola in her female clothing and his request, 'Give me thy hand' (line 270), suggests that he and Viola will soon be married.

Olivia is given Malvolio's letter which is read aloud. The Duke says it does not sound like the letter of a madman and Olivia orders him to be released and brought before her. While waiting for Malvolio Olivia suggests that she and Sebastian, Orsino and Viola should have a double wedding, in public and at her house. To this they all agree.

Malvolio comes in, shows Olivia the letter he had found on the garden path and asks her why she had tricked him in such a manner. Olivia admits that the handwriting closely resembles hers but she recognises it as Maria's. She sympathises with Malvolio and promises that he will have justice. At this point, Fabian confesses his part in the plot to trick Malvolio. He claims that it was Sir Toby's idea to humiliate Malvolio and adds that Sir Toby had been so pleased with Maria's ruse that he had since married her. Malvolio refuses to be reconciled with the others and goes off claiming: 'I'll be revenged on the whole pack of you' (line 377).

Olivia acknowledges that Malvolio has been badly treated but her regret cannot tinge the happiness of the occasion and there is even hope that Malvolio will be placated because the Duke sends an attendant after him to: '. . . entreat him to a peace.' (line 379).

The play ends, as it began, with music, a traditional symbol of peace and order, as Feste sings of the various stages in a man's life.

NOTES AND GLOSSARY:

let me see his letter: the letter is the one written to Olivia by Malvolio

conclusions to be as kisses: the meaning of the Clown's statement seems to be that four negatives make two affirmatives just as four lips make two mouths and two mouths can make one kiss

the old saying is, the third pays for all: the Clown has now received two tips and asks for a third suggesting that in many games it is true to say that one is lucky the third time

That face of his I do remember well . . .: the Duke recognises Antonio and explains how Antonio was the captain of a small ship of very little value and yet he attacked and overcame the best ship in Orsino's fleet. Antonio's behaviour was so brave that even his enemies admired him

this is that Antonio That took the Phoenix: this line means that Antonio had captured the *Phoenix* and its cargo when it was on its way from Candia in Crete

desperate of shame and state: the officer explains that Antonio seemed to care nothing about his own safety and had been arrested for taking part in a street brawl

witchcraft: in this line the word is to be interpreted as meaning 'a very strong attraction'. Antonio suggests that his affection for Sebastian was misplaced

wrack: a lost or ruined person or thing

his false cunning . . . Taught him to face me out of his acquaintance: Antonio cannot understand how such a young man could have become so cunning that he had the audacity to deny all knowledge of Antonio

Cesario, you do not keep promise with me: Olivia is surprised to see that Cesario is still in the Duke's service and so she rebukes him for breaking 'his' promise to her

It is as fat and fulsome to my ear: Olivia does not want to hear the Duke's proposals which she finds as distasteful as ever. His proposal is as unwelcome to her as is the howling of a dog after one has been listening to music

Why should I not . . . Kill what I love: Thyamis, an Egyptian robber, is reported to have tried to kill the woman he loved rather than lose her. The Duke suggests that Olivia's behaviour might encourage him to kill her. Nevertheless, he decides that it would be better revenge to let Olivia live but to kill Cesario who has won Olivia's heart but also caused the Duke to love 'him'

it is the baseness of thy fear: Olivia suggests that Cesario has denied their betrothal because of his fear of the Duke

joinder: joining

O thou dissembling cub!: the fox is renowned for its cunning. The Duke calls Cesario a 'young fox' and wonders what 'he' will be like when 'his' hair is grey. But perhaps Cesario's deceit will bring about 'his' downfall before 'he' grows much older

Hold little faith, though thou hast too much fear: Olivia tells Cesario that, in spite of his fear, he should be more faithful and loyal to her

coxcomb: the word 'coxcomb' was sometimes used to mean 'head', as it is here, but its more usual meaning is 'fool', as in line 204 of this scene

othergates: in a different way

sot: fool and drunkard

Then he's a rogue, and a passy measures pavin: Sir Toby suggests that if the doctor was drunk at eight o'clock in the morning, then he is not a good or honest man. In referring to 'passy measures pavin' Sir Toby is probably comparing the walk of a drunken man with the movement of a dancer

perspective: a distorting glass. The Duke is claiming that to have two people so alike must be a distortion of Nature

Fear'st thou that Antonio?: Sebastian assures Antonio that he is indeed Sebastian by asking Antonio if he could be in doubt as to his (Sebastian's) identity

till each circumstance Of place, time, fortune do cohere: Viola means 'till each detail of place, time and fortune holds together and fits perfectly'

A spirit I am indeed: Sebastian agrees he is a spirit, but his spirit has, since his birth, been attached to the same body

You are betrothed both to a maid and man: Sebastian claims that Olivia is now betrothed to a young man who is a virgin

If this be so, as yet the glass seems true: if, the Duke suggests, they are not witnessing an optical illusion, then he too will find good luck because of the shipwreck. By this he means he will have found Viola

And all those sayings, will I over swear: Viola again swears her love for the Duke. She will love him forever. This is the implication of her remark that her love will last as long as the sun's warmth lasts

enlarge: set free

From my remembrance clearly banished his: Olivia admits that her own worries made her forget Malvolio's problem

he holds Belzebub at the stave's end: the Clown admits that Malvolio is not possessed, but keeps the devil at a distance

vox: (*Latin*) voice. The Clown claims the right to read the letter in whatever voice he chooses

Your master quits you: the Duke releases Cesario from his service

geck: fool, idiot

gull: silly fool

upon: on account of

pluck on: cause, provoke

poor fool: this phrase was meant to console, not insult. It is the equivalent of the modern 'poor fellow'

some have greatness thrown upon them: the Clown does not quote Malvolio exactly but uses 'thrown' instead of 'thrust'

interlude: the term was often applied to a short play, or a game of make-believe

convents: is convenient. The Duke is suggesting that when the best time is chosen they will be able to celebrate the weddings

Orsino's mistress and his fancy's queen: Duke Orsino calls Viola his 'fancy's queen' meaning 'the queen of his heart'

Concluding comments

Twelfth Night like most Elizabethan plays has five acts. This was the conventional number of acts in a play and allowed the writer scope to present a story comprehensively. The number of scenes in a play was less conventionalised and might range from fifteen to twenty-five. In *Twelfth Night* there are eighteen scenes and they perform several functions. They provide contrast, help to advance the action, create or modify the atmosphere, show the development of characters, allow characters to move from one place to another and most important of all, perhaps, can suggest that time has passed between the scenes.

As well as following traditions regarding the division of his play into acts and scenes, Shakespeare's use of ejaculations, oaths and references to God was also conventionalised. On 27 May 1606 a statute was passed to prevent swearing in plays. According to the statute one could be fined up to £10 (a great deal of money in Elizabethan times) for using profanely the name of God, of Jesus Christ, of the Holy Ghost or of the Trinity. Shakespeare probably revised *Twelfth Night* after this statute was passed, deleting some references to God or substituting alternative forms. Thus we have references to Mercury:

> Now Mercury endue thee with leasing (that is 'May Mercury teach you to tell lies') (I.5.97)

to Jove by Malvolio in II.5.173: Jove, I thank thee

and by Sir Toby in IV.2.12: Jove bless thee, Master Parson

as well as the use of exclamations which are not immediately obvious as swearing, for example:

> 'Slight (God's light) in II.5.33
> Save thee (God save thee) in III.1.1

and: 'Slid (God's eyelid) in III.4.400.

Shakespeare borrowed many elements in his play from other sources but he dealt with the subject matter in a unique way. There are three inter-related plots in *Twelfth Night* all sharing similar features and all woven together into a well-integrated play. The first plot involves the love interests of Orsino and Olivia, Viola and Sebastian. The second overlaps the first in that it deals with the shipwreck of Viola and Sebastian and relates the story of the twins and the people who befriended them. The third chiefly involves Malvolio, Sir Toby, Sir Andrew and the Clown. This plot is related to the other two by familial and social ties and by the interests and motives of the members of the group. Neither Malvolio nor Sir Andrew thinks of love with the romantic fervour that Orsino does, but their desire to marry Olivia is just as keen. Feste, the Clown, is a further means of linking the plots. He moves from one group to another and is a frequent visitor in the households of both Orsino and Olivia. It is almost as if he, the Clown, symbolises the notion that folly is universal. His importance in the design of the play is stressed by the fact that his song concludes the action. This song suggests that life has gone on for a very long time, that many changes have taken place in the world but human behaviour remains essentially the same.

Part 3

Commentary

Romantic love

Since so much of the action of *Twelfth Night* revolves around the results of falling in love, it may be useful to comment on prevalent Elizabethan attitudes to love, sex and marriage. In Europe, from early Christian times onwards sexual fulfilment was seen by some as healthy, animal enjoyment and by others as bestial, almost shameful, though permissible within the bonds of marriage. Marriage, especially among the wealthy, was usually arranged to strengthen alliances and to extend land holdings rather than to ensure the personal happiness of the individuals getting married. In consequence, sex and love tended to be separated and the tradition of 'courtly love' developed. This tradition idealised love and the role of the woman. It held the view that love between a man and a woman could be purifying and rewarding. It could be spiritual as well as physical. A man could offer his love to a lady and if he behaved with dignity and decorum over a reasonable period of time, the lady might then reward his constancy by taking him as a lover.

The concept of courtly love affected European literature from about the twelfth century onward and affected those who read the literature. There is a trace of this love in the Duke's attitude to Olivia. He loves her not as a man loves a woman but as a worshipper might adore a goddess:

Tell her my love, more noble than the world,
Prizes not quantity of dirty lands;
The parts that fortune hath bestow'd upon her,
Tell her I hold as giddily as fortune:
But 'tis that miracle and queen of gems
That nature pranks [that is, adorns] her in, attracts my soul.
    (II.4.82–7)

Romantic love resembled courtly love in that it too tended to idealise the beloved. It differed, however, in that romantic love was normally based on physical attraction and often led to marriage. Romantic love figures prominently in such Shakespearean plays as *Romeo and Juliet* and in *Twelfth Night* we have three recorded instances of love at first sight. The Duke describes his attraction to Olivia thus:

> O, when mine eyes did see Olivia first,
> Methought she purg'd the air of pestilence;
> That instant was I turned into a hart,
> And my desires, like fell and cruel hounds,
> E'er since pursue me.
> > (I.1.19–23)

Viola barely knows the Duke when she realises she loves him and must carry his love messages to another woman:

> I'll do my best
> To woo your lady: yet, a barful strife!
> Who'er I woo, myself would be his wife.
> > (I.4.40–2)

and Olivia realises that she loves 'Cesario' after having seen him only once:

> Even so quickly may one catch the plague?
> Methinks I feel this youth's perfections
> With an invisible and subtle stealth
> To creep in at mine eyes.
> > (I.5.299–302)

It is almost as if Shakespeare is underlining the view expressed by Marlowe in his poem *Hero and Leander*:

> Where both deliberate, the love is slight
> Who ever loved, that loved not at first sight?

One further Elizabethan view of love should be mentioned, the view that love can be a type of melancholy and thus an illness. In *Twelfth Night* both Orsino and Olivia are 'afflicted' by their love which gives them pain and causes them to behave irrationally.

It is only when a modern reader is aware of the various connotations that 'love' could have for an Elizabethan audience that he can begin to understand Orsino. To a modern reader Orsino's declarations of love for Olivia can sound unmanly, perhaps even unbalanced, but to an Elizabethan audience they would be understood as the expression of emotion by a young man who had read too much literature and who had fallen in love with the idea of love.

Character evaluation

Shakespeare's characters are usually subtly drawn. Like living human beings they are rarely completely good or completely bad, and can show different sides of their nature depending on the people they are with or the circumstances in which they find themselves. In evaluating the characters in *Twelfth Night*, therefore, one should:

(*a*) avoid sweeping generalisations

(*b*) try to support one's opinions by reference to and quotation from the play

(*c*) consider the character's own words and actions but also give weight to what other characters in the play say about him.

It is necessary to realise that a character is capable of changing. It would thus be unfair to judge a character by first impressions, however important these might be.

Viola

Viola is young, beautiful, loving, intelligent and generous. Her brother described her as:

A lady . . . (who) was . . . of many accounted beautiful: . . . (and) she bore a mind that envy could but call fair.
(II.1.24–9)

Her good looks are also commented on by the Duke:

Diana's lip
Is not more smooth and rubious: thy small pipe [that is, voice]
Is as the maiden's organ, shrill and sound, [that is, pure and unbroken]
(I.4.31–3)

by Olivia (I.5.300) and even by Malvolio who rarely praised anyone and yet he refers to Viola as 'well-favoured' (I.5.162).

Viola is perhaps the most attractive character in the play. She is central to the action and is instrumental in linking the plots involving the court and the shipwreck (see p.47). She is practical and well-balanced. Both she and Olivia have lost brothers they love. Olivia's reaction is to go into mourning whereas Viola makes plans to disguise herself and find employment at the Duke's court (I.2.53–5). Viola's disguise involved her in playing the part of a young courtier throughout most of the action, and she played the role with skill. Like the Duke, she is musical:

I can sing,
And speak to him in many sorts of music, [that is, and play several
instruments]
(I.2.57–8)

She has a strong sense of duty and loyalty. Even though she loves Orsino and would like to be his wife, she does her best to win Olivia for him. Nor does she show any dislike of Olivia. Indeed, she pities Olivia when she falls in love with herself in the guise of Cesario and does not reveal to Malvolio that Olivia has indiscreetly sent a love offering of a ring to a page (see II.2). When Viola finds herself surrounded by problems, she refuses to be depressed by them feeling that solutions will come in time:

> O time, thou must untangle this, not I,
> It is too hard a knot for me t'untie.
> (II.2.39–40)

The audience and the reader sympathise with Viola when she finds herself in a dilemma because of being challenged to a duel. Her fear almost causes her to reveal her disguise:

> Pray God defend me! A little thing would make me tell them how much I lack of a man.
> (III.4.307–9)

It is worth stressing that with all her intelligence Viola is as easily tricked by Sir Toby and Fabian as Malvolio was, and falls in love as quickly as Olivia does. The difference between their reactions to falling in love is that Viola does not reveal her love openly though in her discussion of love with Orsino she takes the opportunity to tell him how constant and enduring a woman's love can be (see II.4., esp. 105ff).

Orsino

Duke Orsino is young, moody, and a good ruler. The sea-captain describes him to Viola as: 'A noble duke, in nature as in name' (I.2.25). And Olivia while refusing his marriage proposals can acknowledge his gifts:

> Your lord does know my mind, I cannot love him.
> Yet I suppose him virtuous, know him noble,
> Of great estate, of fresh and stainless youth;
> In voices well divulg'd, free, learn'd, and valiant,
> And in dimension, and the shape of nature,
> A gracious person.
> (I.5.261–6)

Orsino is cultured. His love of music is well-known. Our first introduction to the play and the Duke involves a reference to music: 'If music be the food of love, play on' (I.1.1), and he rewards the Clown handsomely in Act II, Scene 4 for his excellent singing. His use of language tends to be literary and he seems to take pleasure in the poetic nature of his utterances:

> Mark it, Cesario, it is old and plain;
> The spinsters and the knitters in the sun,
> And the free maids that weave their thread with bones
> Do use to chant it:
>   (II.4.43–6)

Orsino's love for Olivia suggests his immaturity. His love is idealised and sentimental in contrast to the genuine affection he develops for Cesario. Orsino appears almost to take pleasure in the pain of unfulfilled love. He was content to send messengers to plead his case to Olivia for the majority of the action of the play and only went in person once. The language used by Orsino to describe his love is a little disturbing. He describes it as being: '. . . as hungry as the sea' (II.4.101), and he can contemplate killing a loved one:

> I'll sacrifice the lamb that I do love,
> To spite a raven's heart within a dove.
>   (V.1.128–9)

but we can ascribe such descriptions in part to his immaturity and injured pride and in part to his frequent use of imagery-laden language.

Orsino's moodiness is again partly due to youthful inexperience. The Clown sums up this aspect of the Duke's character by saying:

> . . . the tailor make thy doublet of changeable taffeta, for thy mind is very opal.
>   (II.4.74–5)

Nevertheless, in spite of the Duke's weaknesses, we should remember the good opinion others have of him, his ability to admire a brave enemy (for example his praise of Antonio in V.1.49ff) and the fact that he is capable of self-correction, of learning to give up his idealised love for Olivia in order to devote his life and affection to Viola.

Olivia

Olivia is a beautiful countess. The Duke eulogises: 'Here comes the Countess: now heaven walks on earth' (V.1.95), and Viola admits:

> I see you what you are, you are too proud:
> But if you were the devil, you are fair.
>   (I.5.254–5)

She is young and virtuous. The sea-captain describes her as:

> A virtuous maid, the daughter of a count
> That died some twelvemonth since;
>   (I.2.36–7)

and her youthful inexperience is suggested by her sentimental grief and her vow to mourn for seven years. Both her grief and her vow are put aside as soon as she falls in love with Cesario. In spite of her youth, however, she is capable of inspiring the respect of her household. Sebastian admires the way she is able to:

> ... sway her house, command her followers,
> Take and give back affairs and their dispatch,
> With such a smooth, discreet, and stable bearing
> (IV.3.17–19)

Olivia is a good judge of character. She recognises the falseness of Orsino's declaration of love: '... it is heresy' (I.5.231), and she values Malvolio's virtues even though she is aware of his basic weakness: 'O, you are sick of self-love, Malvolio' (I.5.89).

Olivia is also capable of judging her own actions. She recognises the inadvisability of her love for Cesario and tries to overcome it:

> I have said too much unto a heart of stone,
> And laid mine honour too unchary out:
> There's something in me that reproves my fault:
> (III.4.203–5)

yet she knows her own weakness and tells Cesario: 'A friend like thee might bear my soul to hell' (III.4.219). Her love proves to be greater than her pride and she is willing to offer herself and her fortune to someone she thought was a page: 'Nor wit nor reason can my passion hide' (III.1.154).

Olivia is also a woman of action. As soon as she realises the depth of her feeling for Cesario she takes steps to win 'his' love and bind 'him' in marriage.

Olivia is loyal to people who have served her well. She shows solicitude for Malvolio when she thinks he is mad and is upset to learn how he was tricked and ill-used:

> Alas, Malvolio, ...
> ... Prithee, be content;
> This practice hath most shrewdly pass'd upon thee.
> But when we know the ground and authors of it,
> Thou shalt be both the plaintiff and the judge
> Of thine own cause.
> (V.1.344–53)

She also has a sense of humour and, in spite of her grief, can bandy words with the Clown (see I.5.30–80).

Olivia is self-willed and immature. Her grief is as sentimental as Orsino's love but, like Orsino, she changes as circumstances change.

Sebastian

Sebastian is young, active, brave and affectionate. He plays an important part in *Twelfth Night* as far as the development of the plot is concerned and yet his appearances in the play are limited. One of the reasons why the reader feels he knows Sebastian so well is that he closely resembles Viola both in person and in character. Our first introduction to Sebastian stresses his courage and self-reliance. The sea-captain tells Viola:

> I saw your brother,
> Most provident in peril, bind himself
> (Courage and hope both teaching him the practice)
> To a strong mast that liv'd [that is, floated] upon the sea;
> Where, like Arion on the dolphin's back,
> I saw him hold acquaintance with the waves
> So long as I could see.
>   (I.2.11–17)

Sebastian is affectionate as a brother (read what he says of Viola in II.1.24–31) and as a friend:

> Antonio! O my dear Antonio,
> How have the hours rack'd and tortur'd me,
> Since I have lost thee!
>   (V.1.216–8)

Indeed, it says much for Sebastian's attractiveness that he could have inspired such deep affection in Antonio after such a short time.

Sebastian is a man of action in contrast to the Duke who is more a man of words. He responds immediately to the challenge of a fight with Sir Andrew and Sir Toby but he does not like violence and apologises to Olivia for having hurt her kinsman:

> I am sorry, madam, I have hurt your kinsman:
> But had it been the brother of my blood,
> I must have done no less with wit and safety.
>   (V.1.207–9)

He responds equally fast to Olivia's offer of love and marriage and yet we feel that his decision:

> I'll . . . go with you,
> And having sworn truth, ever will be true
>   (IV.3.32–3)

is based on a rapid assessment of Olivia's character rather than on rash impulse.

Antonio

Antonio's main role in the play is to reveal facets of Sebastian's character. The young man inspires a deep affection in Antonio:

> I have many enemies in Orsino's court,
> Else would I very shortly see thee there:
> But come what may, I do adore thee so,
> That danger shall seem sport, and I will go.
> (II.1.44–7)

Antonio is generous. He gives Sebastian his purse in case the young man sees something he might like:

> Haply your eye shall light upon some toy [that is, some trifle]
> You have desire to purchase:
> (III.3.44–5)

and his bravery is beyond question. He immediately goes to the aid of Sebastian when he thinks he is duelling with Sir Andrew (see III.4.319ff) and although he had been an enemy of the Duke's, Antonio's courage was admired:

> A baubling vessel was he captain of,
> For shallow draught and bulk unprizable,
> With which such scathful grapple did he make
> With the most noble bottom of our fleet,
> That very envy and the tongue of loss
> Cried fame and honour on him.
> (V.1.52–7)

Malvolio

Malvolio is probably the most complex character in *Twelfth Night*. The audience laughs at him and yet, at the same time, sympathises with him. In Act V when he is allowed to explain how he was tricked he does so with dignity and without self-pity. It is well to remember that his desire to marry Olivia is not as ludicrous as it might first appear. He was not a menial servant but was steward of an important household and had probably been a member of the lower gentry. Certainly Olivia does not seem shocked to learn that he had hoped to marry her.

Malvolio was a conscientious, efficient steward who was highly prized by Olivia who would, in her own words, prefer to lose half her wealth than have anything go wrong with Malvolio: 'I would not have him miscarry for the half of my dowry' (III.4.62–3). His power as a steward caused him, on occasions, to behave arrogantly. His attitude to Sir Toby's revelling is intentionally offensive:

> My masters, are you mad? Or what are you? Have you no wit,
> manners, nor honesty, but to gabble like tinkers at this time of night?
> (II.3.87–9)

and a similar sort of arrogance is seen in the way he returns the ring
to Cesario:

> If it be worth stooping for, there it lies, in your eye: if not, be it his
> that finds it.
> (II.2.13–15)

Maria is prejudiced against Malvolio and we must remember this when
we judge her description of him. She comments on his vanity and
hypocrisy:

> ... he is ... a time-pleaser, an affectioned ass, that cons state without
> book, and utters it by great swarths: the best persuaded of himself,
> so crammed (as he thinks) with excellencies, that it is his grounds
> of faith that all that look on him love him.
> (II.3.147–52)

Yet Maria knew him well enough to appeal to his personal vanity when
the letter instructed him what clothes to wear:

> Remember who commended thy yellow stockings, and wished to see
> thee ever cross-gartered.
> (II.5.152–4)

Since no devout Puritan would have worn yellow stockings there is
some truth in Maria's claims. In addition, Maria's criticisms gain
credence from the fact that he was disliked by all the members of
Olivia's household that we meet. Fabian, for example, tells us that he
took part in the plot against Malvolio because of Malvolio's 'stubborn
and uncourteous parts' (V.1.360).

Malvolio lacks a sense of humour and is unable to appreciate the
Clown. Olivia criticises his cheerless nature:

> O, you are sick of self-love, Malvolio, and taste with a distempered
> appetite. To be generous, guiltless, and of free disposition, is to take
> those things for bird-bolts that you deem cannon-bullets.
> (I.5.89–93)

though she valued his gravity at times:

> Where's Malvolio? He is sad and civil,
> And suits well for a servant with my fortunes:
> (III.4.5–6)

Malvolio seems most sympathetic when he is most afflicted. One admires his courage and constancy to his religious principles when he argues so valiantly with the mock-priest Sir Topas. In spite of his weaknesses and Maria's criticisms of him because he is 'a kind of Puritan' (II.3.140) the reader tends to agree with Olivia's assessment that: 'He hath been most notoriously abus'd' (V.1.378).

Reference has already been made (see p.9) to the fact that, in the Elizabethan period, Puritans were opposed to drama. Consequently, some critics of *Twelfth Night* have assumed that in creating Malvolio Shakespeare was making fun of Puritans. If we examine the character of Malvolio closely, however, we would probably have to decide that, in Malvolio, Shakespeare was satirising vanity and hypocrisy, which are human, rather than exclusively Puritan, weaknesses.

Maria

Maria is Olivia's gentlewoman and so not a mere servant. She is pretty, intelligent, well-educated—she can write and imitate Olivia's writing—and she is fond of fun. She dislikes Malvolio and is responsible for thinking up and organising a plot to hurt his pride and sense of self-importance:

> For Monsieur Malvolio, let me alone with him. If I do not . . . make him a common recreation [that is, a laughing-stock for everyone], do not think I have wit enough to lie straight in my bed:
> (II.3.134–8)

She likes Sir Toby who refers to her as 'one that adores me' (II.3.179–80) and she achieves two objectives by the skill of her plot. She humiliates Malvolio and marries Sir Toby. Maria can inspire affection and loyalty in others. Sir Toby marries her and Fabian defends her action when he tells Olivia why Malvolio was so badly treated:

> Most freely I confess, myself and Toby
> Set this device against Malvolio here,
> Upon some stubborn and uncourteous parts
> We had conceived against him. Maria writ
> The letter, at Sir Toby's great importance,
> In recompense whereof he hath married her.
> (V.1.358–63)

Sir Toby Belch

Sir Toby's surname suggests over-indulgence and he lives up to his name in that, whenever we meet him in the play, he is either drinking or drunk. He shares characteristics with the country squires of much subsequent literature (Squire Western in *Tom Jones* (1749), for example) in that he is very fond of drinking revelling and playing practical jokes. His exact relationship with Olivia is not stated, but the use of such kinship terms as 'uncle' and 'niece' suggest that he is older than Olivia. This need not mean, however, that he is an old man. Indeed, the speed with which he enters duels and later marries Maria would suggest that he is still a virile man.

Sir Toby is something of a parasite. He lives at ease in Olivia's house and cheats Sir Andrew out of a lot of his money. As Sir Toby explains to Fabian: 'I have been dear [that is, costly] to him, lad, some two thousand strong, or so' (III.2.52–3).

Sir Toby is invariably cheerful. As he explains it: 'I am sure care's an enemy of life' (I.3.2–3). He is brave, being prepared to fight both Antonio and Sebastian, and he admires Maria's intelligence. He is quite shrewd when it comes to judging human weaknesses. He realises that Sir Andrew is a complete coward, that Cesario is afraid of duelling, that Maria is fond of him and that Malvolio lacks human understanding. His question to Malvolio:

> Dost thou think because thou art virtuous, there shall be no more cakes and ale?
> (II.3.114–15)

pinpoints Malvolio's lack of tolerance.

Sir Toby has many weaknesses. He is a drunkard, a bully and a cheat but his wit and courage do much to redeem him in the eyes of the audience.

Sir Andrew Aguecheek

As with Sir Toby, Sir Andrew's surname, suggesting one who is lean and cowardly, marks him out as a comic character. He is cowardly, ignorant and quarrelsome. Maria aptly sums him up when she says:

> . . . besides that he's a fool, he's a great quarreller, and but that he hath the gift of a coward to allay the gust [that is, gusto] he hath in quarrelling, 'tis thought among the prudent he would quickly have the gift of a grave.
> (I.3.30–3)

Sir Andrew is easily led by Sir Toby whom he admires and imitates:

SIR TOBY: Excellent, I smell a device.
SIR ANDREW: I have't in my nose too.
(II.3.163–4)

SIR TOBY: I could marry this wench for this device.
SIR ANDREW: So could I too.
SIR TOBY: And ask no other dowry with her but such another jest.
SIR ANDREW: Nor I neither.
          (II.5.182–6)

He never realises that Sir Toby has cheated him and remains loyal to Sir Toby throughout, even telling Cesario that Sir Toby would have defeated 'him' had it not been for his drunken condition: '. . . if he had not been in drink, he would have tickled you othergates than he did' (V.1.191–2). Like many cowards, Sir Andrew is a bully. As soon as he thinks Cesario is afraid of him he determines to follow 'him' and beat 'him': ' 'Slid, I'll after him again, and beat him' (III.4.400).

Fabian

Fabian is another member of Olivia's household whose exact rank is not known. Judging by his actions and by his familiarity with Sir Toby it would appear that he, too, is a member of the lower gentry. He is happy and eager to enjoy a practical joke:

> I will not give my part of this sport for a pension of thousands to be paid from the Sophy.
>   (II.5.180–1)

He has some reason for disliking Malvolio in that:

> . . . he brought me out o' favour with my lady [Olivia], about a bear-baiting here.
>   (II.5.6–8)

He supports Sir Toby and Maria in their practical joke on Malvolio and tries to defend Maria when in Act V, Scene 1, 354–66 he reveals how Malvolio has been tricked. He was not being disloyal to Sir Toby when he blamed Sir Toby rather than Maria for thinking up the plot. After all, Sir Toby was Olivia's kinsman and so could not be reprimanded in the same way as an ordinary member of the household could.

Feste, the Clown

In Tudor times, a 'fool' or 'jester' was a salaried member of many palaces and stately homes. Their role was to entertain and amuse. Frequently they wore a multicoloured outfit (referred to as 'motley') and a cap with small bells attached. Shakespeare often introduces a 'clown' or 'fool' into his plays. In these, they serve the purpose of

amusing and entertaining the audience, sometimes by singing, but for
Shakespeare they had an additional role. They were used to express a
Shakespearean belief that folly is universal and that wisdom is often
found in the mouth of a fool.

Feste is a professional fool and he shows none of the unintelligent
folly of Sir Andrew Aguecheek. He is a fine musician and he takes
pleasure in music as he tells the Duke in Act II, Scene 4, 68: 'I take
pleasure in singing, sir.' He has considerable insight into human nature.
He sings love songs for the Duke, and boisterous songs for the fun-
loving Sir Toby. His knowledge of people has made him aware that
wisdom and folly are often found in the same person:

> Those wits [that is, wise men] that think they have thee [that is,
> wisdom], do very oft prove fools: and I that am sure I lack thee
> [wisdom], may pass for a wise man.
> (I.5.31–3)

Feste seems to be keenly interested in money and is prepared to flatter
in order to get it:

> By my troth, thou hast an open hand. These wise men that give fools
> money get themselves a good report—after fourteen years' purchase.
> (IV.1.21–3)

He also manages to get money from the Duke, Viola and Sir Toby.
Feste seems well-disposed towards everyone in the play except Malvolio
but he is most interested in his own welfare and in keeping his position
with Olivia. His instinct for self-preservation overrides his loyalty to
Sir Toby and Sir Andrew because, when he sees them about to attack
Sebastian whom they all believe to be Cesario, he says: 'This will I tell
my lady straight: I would not be in some of your coats for twopence'
(IV.1.29–30).

Feste's witty remarks are planned and polished as are his songs. He
helps to link the various sub-plots (see earlier comments, on p.47) and
is responsible for a good deal of the humour and musical pleasure that
the play gives.

Poetic language

The creative writer enjoys considerable freedom in his use of language
in that he can mould it to suit his literary purposes. Poetic language
derives from ordinary everyday speech but it differs from everyday
speech in that its purpose is not merely to communicate facts but also to
delight and impress by exploiting the resources of the language to the
full. Poetry differs from literary prose in that it is rhythmically regular.

It is possible to compare, for example, the regular stress pattern of :

> That strain again, it had a dying fall:
> O, it came o'er my ear like the sweet sound
> That breathes upon a bank of violets,
> Stealing and giving odour. Enough, no more;
> 'Tis not so sweet now as it was before.
> (I.1.4–8)

with the more speech-like prose statement of Fabian:

> She did show favour to the youth in your sight only to exasperate you, to awake your dormouse valour, to put fire in your heart, and brimstone in your liver.
> (III.2.16–19)

Imagery

The use of images is basic to all vivid language and can occur in poetry and prose alike. In *Twelfth Night* we find recurrent images of the sea:

> O spirit of love, how quick and fresh art thou,
> That notwithstanding thy capacity
> Receiveth as the sea
> (I.1.9–11)

of flowers:

> For women are as roses, whose fair flower
> Being once display'd, doth fall that very hour
> (II.4.38–9)

of precious stones:

> The tailor make thy doublet of changeable taffeta, for thy mind is very opal
> (II.4.74–5)

of animals and birds:

> I'll sacrifice the lamb that I do love,
> To spite a raven's heart within a dove
> (V.1.128–9)

of hunting, when Fabian describes Malvolio falling for Maria's trick:

> Now is the woodcock near the gin [that is, the trap]
> (II.5.84)

Other images abound in the play and it might be useful to examine the type of imagery used by individual characters.

Simile and metaphor

These are often found in literary language because they allow the writer to extend the range of his references. If Shakespeare, for example, says that love is like war or like the sea, he can then use images of war and of the sea when referring to love. Similes and metaphors involve comparisons. With similes, the comparison is overt. We say that one thing is like another or has some of the qualities of something else. Thus the sea-captain uses a simile when he compares Sebastian with Arion:

> I saw your brother,
> Most provident in peril, bind himself
>   . . . .
> To a strong mast that liv'd upon the sea;
> Where, like Arion on the dolphin's back,
> I saw him hold acquaintance with the waves
>   (I.2.11–16)

The Duke uses another when he claims that the effect of the music is not as pleasant as it was previously:

> 'Tis not so sweet now as it was before.
>   (I.1.8)

and two examples occur in Viola's description of unrequited love:

>   she never told her love,
> But let concealment like a worm i' th' bud
> Feed on her damask cheek: she pin'd in thought,
> And with a green and yellow melancholy
> She sat like Patience on a monument,
> Smiling at grief.
>   (II.4.111–16)

With metaphor, the comparison is implied rather than stated. When, in *Macbeth*, Shakespeare wrote of the brevity of life as resembling the brief existence of a candle which can be put out at any moment, he was using metaphor. Metaphors are used in all varieties of language and numerous examples can be found in *Twelfth Night*. In Act I, Scene 5, 242–3, Viola uses a metaphor when she personifies Nature:

> 'Tis beauty truly blent, whose red and white
> Nature's own sweet and cunning hand laid on.

So does Fabian, comparing Sir Andrew's bravery to that of a dormouse:

> She did show favour to the youth . . . to awake your dormouse valour
>   (III.2.16–18)

The Duke's speech contains many metaphors. One can, for example, find two in the following extract where he compares Cesario with a cunning fox-cub and speaks of time as if it had human properties:

> O thou dissembling cub! What wilt thou be
> When time hath sow'd a grizzle on thy case? [that is, when time has put grey hairs on your body]
> (V.1.162–3)

Word play

Playing on different meanings of the same word or on words which have the same sound has been popular in English literature since the time of Chaucer. Shakespeare and his contemporaries employed word play as a literary technique and also for the amusement and intellectual pleasure it seems to have given their audience. Examples of word play can be found throughout the play. In Act I, Scene 1, 18–23, the Duke plays on the similarity of pronunciation between a 'hart' which is a hunted animal and his 'heart', the seat of his love for Olivia:

> O, when mine eyes did see Olivia first,
> Methought she purged the air of pestilence;
> That instant was I turned into a hart,
> And my desires, like fell and cruel hounds,
> E'er since pursue me.

Later, in Act II, Scene 1, 29–31, Sebastian plays on the two meanings of 'salt water', the 'sea' and 'tears':

> She is drowned already, sir, with salt water, though I seem to drown her remembrance again with more.

And in Act III, Scene 2, 51–3, there is punning on the two meanings of 'dear', that is 'well-liked' and 'costly':

> FABIAN: This is a dear manikin to you, Sir Toby.
> SIR TOBY: I have been dear to him, lad, some two thousand strong or so.

Dramatic irony

The term 'dramatic irony' is applied to an episode in a play where the audience can see more significance in the words of a character than the other characters can. In Act I, Scene 5, 185, for example, when Viola in the guise of Cesario says: 'I am not that I play' [that is, I am not the person I seem to be], Olivia interprets the statement as meaning that Cesario is of noble birth whereas the audience knows 'he' is Viola dressed as a page and the entire conversation between the Duke and Viola in Act II, Scene 4, 79–125, can be interpreted on two levels because only the audience and Viola are aware of Viola's disguise.

Concluding comments

In literature, characters are presented by means of what they say and what they do. It may be useful, therefore, to summarise the events of the play showing how the characters interact. There is a problem involved in deciding how much time is covered by the action of the play. At first, it appears to take place on three days with a three-day interval in between and yet, in Act V, Scene 1, 97, the Duke claims that Viola has been in his service for three months. Such discrepancies are not uncommon in Shakespeare and would almost certainly not be noticed in a performance.

Day 1, covering Act I, Scenes 1–3

(*i*) Duke Orsino learns that his messenger has been unsuccessful in persuading Olivia to return the Duke's love.

(*ii*) Viola and her twin brother, Sebastian, are shipwrecked. Viola is saved by the sea-captain and, without her knowledge, Sebastian is saved by Antonio. Viola dresses as a page and goes to Illyria to serve the Duke.

(*iii*) Sir Toby persuades Sir Andrew that Olivia may marry him (Sir Andrew) and Sir Andrew joins Olivia's household.

At this point it would appear that there is a three-day interval because in Scene 4 Valentine tells Cesario that the Duke: '. . . hath known you but three days' (I.4.2–3).

Day 2, covering Act I, Scenes 4–5 and Act II, Scenes 1–3

(*iv*) The Duke asks Cesario to be his messenger of love to Olivia. Cesario agrees in spite of the fact that 'he' has fallen in love with Orsino.

(*v*) Olivia falls in love with Cesario.

ACT II

(*i*) Antonio and Sebastian decide to visit Illyria.

(*ii*) Olivia sends a ring to Cesario as a token of her love.

(*iii*) Malvolio reprimands Sir Toby for revelling and he and Maria decide that Malvolio must be humiliated.

Day 3, covering Act II, Scene 4 to Act V, Scene 1

(*iv*) Once again the Duke sends Cesario to plead his case to Olivia.
(*v*) Malvolio is tricked into believing that Olivia loves him.

ACT III
(*i*) Olivia tells Cesario that she loves 'him'.
(*ii*) Sir Andrew sees how fond Olivia is of Cesario and is advised by Sir Toby and Fabian to challenge Cesario to a duel.
(*iii*) Sebastian and Antonio arrive in the city and separate for Antonio's greater safety.
(*iv*) Malvolio has been completely taken in by Maria's forged letter; Cesario is forced into the duel with Sir Andrew and is rescued by Antonio who thinks Cesario is Sebastian; Antonio is arrested for an earlier crime of piracy.

ACT IV
(*i*) The Clown mistakes Sebastian for Cesario and so does Olivia; Sebastian agrees to return to Olivia's house with her.
(*ii*) Malvolio is kept in a darkened room because of his supposed madness.
(*iii*) Sebastian and Olivia are betrothed.

ACT V
(*i*) Viola and Sebastian are seen together; Olivia and Sebastian agree to keep their vows and Viola is united with the Duke; Antonio and Malvolio are both released from their confinements and the play ends with Feste's song.

It has sometimes been argued that the final scenes in *Twelfth Night* are not true to life, that the marriage arrangements are too rapid and that Viola and the Duke are not really suited to each other. It is well to remember, however, that marriages end Shakespeare's comedies just as surely as deaths end his tragedies. In addition, one does not look to literature for chronological precision or logical exactness. The only truth that has value in a work of art is a truth which imposes a coherence on the many strands that are woven together by the artist.

Part 4

Hints for study

Studying *Twelfth Night*

In studying any of Shakespeare's plays it is necessary to understand
something of the times in which they were written. To have a knowledge
of the beliefs and concerns of Shakespeare's contemporaries and to be
aware of the changes that the English language has undergone since the
beginning of the seventeenth century will help the reader to appreciate
and enjoy Shakespeare's works. In studying *Twelfth Night*, it is useful
to know the text well and to be able to offer a quotation in support of
your views, but knowledge of sections of the text is less important than
understanding the meaning of the entire play, its literary value and
dramatic worth.

It is also useful to remind yourself that *Twelfth Night* is a play which
was meant to be watched and enjoyed, and not a philosophical essay
whose every comma has significance. The titles *Twelfth Night* or *What
You Will* underline Shakespeare's attitude to his drama. Mirth and
entertainment were suggested by *Twelfth Night* and the sub-title implies
that the audience's pleasure was of paramount importance. The play is
a comedy and humour is to be found in:

(*a*) the scenes of revelry involving Sir Toby and his set

(*b*) the folly of Malvolio's behaviour when he believes that 'greatness
has been thrust upon him'

(*c*) the duel between the cowardly Sir Andrew and the frightened Viola

(*d*) the problems connected with mistaken identity, and in:

(*e*) the wordplay.

To describe *Twelfth Night* as a comedy does not detract from the more
serious issues that arise with regard to the treatment of Malvolio, but
the student is advised to concentrate on the dramatic and musical
delights that *Twelfth Night* can still offer.

Answering questions

There is no set of mechanical rules which a student can follow in order to produce a good answer but an answer will have much to recommend it if the student remembers the following points:

(a) Read the question paper slowly and select the questions you are best able to deal with. Take your time at this stage because the results of your examination will depend on the wisdom of your choice.

(b) Calculate the amount of time you have for each question and try to keep to a time scheme. If the examination is three hours long and there are four questions to answer, then you should ensure that you spend less than forty-five minutes on each question. In most examinations all questions have equal value and it would thus be foolish to lose marks by failing to give any one question adequate time.

(c) Plan your answer in points before writing your essay. If, for example, you are asked to describe Viola's character, it would be useful to prepare such a list as:

intelligent, resourceful, generous, cheerful, attractive, loyal, with a sense of humour and a sense of her own limitations.

before answering the question fully.

(d) Use quotations where possible in support of your opinion. If you wish, for example, to comment on Viola's resourcefulness, it would be of value to quote her decision to disguise herself and serve the Duke:

I prithee . . .
Conceal me what I am, and be my aid
For such disguise as haply shall become
The form of my intent. I'll serve this duke;
Thou shalt present me as an eunuch to him.
It may be worth thy pains; for I can sing,
And speak to him in many sorts of music,
That will allow me very worth his service.
    (I.2.52–9)

The reference to acts, scenes and lines need not be quoted in examinations. They are supplied in these notes to help the student to find the quotations in his own edition and see the context in which they occur. In addition, quotations need not be long. Often, a line or half a line will suffice.

(e) Answer all parts of the question but do not give unnecessary information. If, for example, you are asked to compare the characters of Viola and Olivia, then your answer must allow equal weight to each part. In such a question it would be a waste of time to give a summary of the plot. A good answer gives *all* and *only* the information required.

(f) An answer should be written in the form of an essay. An introductory paragraph should examine the question. Each relevant point should then be dealt with in separate paragraphs and finally, a concluding paragraph should sum up your views on the given subject.

(g) If, in spite of all good intentions, you find that you have misjudged your time and left yourself only a short time to answer your last question, it is advisable to write a good opening paragraph followed by a set of notes showing how your answer would have developed. This alternative is acceptable to most examiners but a complete set of essays is more acceptable still.

(h) Remember that your own style matters. There is no particular merit in long sentences and polysyllabic words. Keep your writing simple, concise and to the point.

(i) Write neatly and legibly. There is little point in presenting information if the examiner cannot read your handwriting.

(j) Always try to leave a few minutes free at the end of an examination to read over your answers and correct any slips.

Specimen questions and suggested answers

It is not always desirable to offer students a set of 'model' answers. In the first place, students are being trained to use their own minds and to offer their own opinions rather than to develop their memories. And secondly, a student who relies on 'model' answers is not likely to use his knowledge creatively. He will find it difficult to select only those pieces of information which are required by the question and so much of his answer may be irrelevant. The intention, throughout these notes, has been to offer ideas and suggestions which the student can think about and transform, rather than to imply that there is only one possible interpretation of any event, or a single view of a character's actions. The student who uses the notes carefully will find in the various sections all the information he needs to write well-balanced answers to the many questions that can be asked about *Twelfth Night*.

It may be useful, however, to indicate how the student might deal with examination questions and so one essay-type answer to a question is presented along with suggested plans for two others. In addition, a set of questions is provided which should be useful for purposes of revision.

Question 1: Samuel Johnson criticised *Twelfth Night* because it lacked credibility and failed to present a true picture of life. Do you agree with Johnson's criticism? Offer reasons for your answer.

PLAN *Introduction:* what is 'credibility'?
Must a drama, to be effective, present a 'true picture of life'?

Body of essay: Aspects of the play which lack credibility
(1) the extreme passion which Orsino expresses for Olivia
(2) the readiness with which Orsino can transfer his love from Olivia to Viola
(3) falling in love at first sight
(4) the speed of Olivia's betrothal to Sebastian
(5) Viola's disguise
(6) the unlikely fact that Viola and Sebastian would be so alike that no one would recognise differences in height, voice or gesture

Aspects of the play that seem true to life
(1) the hopes that can blind one to reality—the hopes that Malvolio and Sir Andrew had of becoming Olivia's husband
(2) the fact that people are complex—Malvolio's courage and Feste's decision to tell tales
(3) the fact that folly and wisdom are not totally separate

Conclusion: weighing up the evidence
Distinguishing between real life and life depicted on the stage
Personal opinion.

ESSAY ANSWER:
Johnson criticised *Twelfth Night* because, as far as he was concerned, certain actions and occurrences in the play bore little resemblance to events in the real world. Anyone who reads the play or thinks about it would have to admit that there is some truth in Johnson's claim, but it is by no means the whole truth. An audience watching a good production of *Twelfth Night* is lulled into a 'willing suspension of their disbelief' because the play has artistic coherence even where it lacks credibility.

Let us first of all examine those aspects of the play that seem most improbable. The Duke's passion for Olivia strikes one as being unrealistic. It is based on physical attraction rather than on knowledge:

O, when mine eyes did see Olivia first,
Methought she purg'd the air of pestilence;
That instant was I turn'd into a hart,
And my desires, like fell hounds,
E'er since pursue me
(I.1.19–23)

and there is a degree of unreality in his behaviour. One might understand a young man being smitten by love but one would not expect him to use intermediaries to express his love. Nor would one expect him to transfer his affection so readily to Viola when he realises that Olivia is already betrothed.

The unreality of the Duke's love is paralleled by the speed with which Viola falls in love with the Duke. After less than three days in his service she admits: 'Whoe'er I woo, myself would be his wife' (I.4.42). There is a similar unlikely haste in Olivia's declaration to Cesario:

Cesario, by the roses of spring,
By maidhood, honour, truth, and everything,
I love thee so, that maugre all thy pride,
Nor wit nor reason can my passion hide
(III.1.151–4)

and in Sebastian's equally hasty acceptance of Olivia's proposal of marriage:

I'll follow this good man [that is, the priest], and go with you,
And having sworn truth, ever will be true.
(IV.3.32–3)

Perhaps two more basic criticisms of the play's lack of credibility relate to Viola's ability to disguise herself so effectively that another woman falls in love with her and to the unlikeliness of twins of different sexes being so alike that no one can tell them apart. The audience is led to believe that no one notices differences in height, voice or gesture. Viola and Sebastian are, in the words of Duke Orsino: 'One face, one voice, one habit, and two persons!' (V.1.214).

When divorced from their context, one might consider that the circumstances and behaviour referred to above fail to present a true picture of life, yet there are many aspects of the play which impress us by their realism. *Twelfth Night* reveals a deep knowledge of human nature with all its complexity and contradictions. We see in the aspirations of Malvolio and Sir Andrew how one's hopes can blind one to one's limitations. We are shown that human beings are complex. Even when we think we know the characters we are capable of being surprised. Just when we are prepared to assess Malvolio as a proud, vain, unsympathetic bigot he shows unexpected courage and dignity, and when we are prepared to acknowledge that Feste is well-disposed to Sir Toby, we see that his sense of self-preservation comes before any feelings of loyalty, with the result that he is even prepared to tell tales on Sir Toby and his friends:

> This will I tell my lady straight: I would not be in some of your coats for twopence.
> (IV.1.29-30)

And there is universal truth in an underlying theme of the play that wisdom and folly are often found together, so that wise men are capable of foolish actions just as wisdom is occasionally found in the words of a fool.

When Johnson said that *Twelfth Night* 'lacked credibility and failed to present a true picture of life' he was drawing attention to the fact that the play has a fairy-tale quality. It tells an unusual story and ends with everyone being happy or having the promise of happiness. But to say this is not to condemn the play. In *Hamlet*, Shakespeare defined the purpose of a play as: '. . . to hold as it were the mirror up to nature' (III.2.21-2), and this would result in a *reflection* rather than a *recreation* of life. Literature idealises life. It tends to impose an order on events, a coherence which is rarely found in day-to-day existence and so, although I accept the validity of Johnson's statement, I do not believe that Shakespeare's 'lack of credibility' or his failure to present 'a true picture of life' should be regarded as flaws.

Question 2: Describe the plot against Malvolio. Why was it so successful?

PLAN *Introduction:* Brief discussion of both parts of the question
Plot was to humiliate Malvolio
It succeeded because of Malvolio's own character and because of the skill with which Maria planned each step

Body of essay: Details of plot against Malvolio:

(1) Maria is aware of Malvolio's vanity, describing him as:

> . . . so crammed (as he thinks) with excellencies, that it is his grounds of faith that all that look on him love him
> (II.3.150-3)

(2) Maria can write like Olivia and she plans to write letters that will convince Malvolio that Olivia loves him

(3) Maria prepares the ground well, suggesting to Malvolio that Olivia was fond of him:

Maria once told me she [that is Olivia] did affect [that is, admire] me (II.5.23-4)

(4) Maria drops letter on path which Malvolio must pass. Letter advises Malvolio to be firm with Sir Toby, to dress more fashionably and not to be afraid of greatness

(5) Malvolio falls for the trick and his behaviour is so strange that Olivia believes he has gone mad

(6) Locked in dark room and tormented by Fabian and Feste

Reasons for the success of the plot:

(1) Malvolio's vanity

(2) The meticulous care with which Maria constructs her plot, suggesting to Malvolio that Olivia likes him before he finds the letter and suggesting to Olivia that Malvolio is mad before Olivia sees him in yellow stockings

(3) Maria and Sir Toby were skilled in the art of practical jokes. It should be remembered that Sir Andrew was also completely fooled by them and Viola was tricked into believing that Sir Andrew was a superb swordsman

Conclusion: The plot against Malvolio was well planned and well executed. It was certainly successful in humiliating Malvolio but Malvolio maintained his dignity under pressure and so the plot did not succeed entirely.

Question 3: What evidence would you offer in defence of the view that Orsino is young and immature?

PLAN *Introduction:* The question presupposes that there is some evidence that Orsino is *not* young and immature. Such evidence would include the facts:

(1) he is an established ruler. The sea-captain refers to him as:

A noble duke, in nature as in name (I.2.25)

(2) he warned Cesario that women of the Duke's age would be too old for Cesario:

DUKE: What kind of woman is't?

. . . .

What years, i' faith?
CESARIO: About your years, my lord.
DUKE: Too old, by heaven!   (II.4.26-9)

(3) he had some time earlier fought a battle at sea with Antonio (see V.1.49–69)

Body of essay: The evidence which suggests Orsino is young and immature:

(1) The intensity of his passion for Olivia

(2) his moodiness, seen in Act I, Scene 1 and commented on by Feste in Act II, Scene 4, 75: '. . . thy mind is very opal'

(3) Olivia refers to him as: '. . . of fresh and stainless youth' (I.5.263)

(4) the passionate extremes expressed in his language:

I'll sacrifice the lamb that I do love,
To spite a raven's heart within a dove
(V.1.128–9)

which are more easily ascribed to the injured pride of youth than to mature reflection

(5) the speed with which he switches his affection from Olivia to Viola

Conclusion: There is some doubt as to the Duke's age because Shakespeare wished to imply that he was:

(1) a good ruler with considerable experience and

(2) a young man in love

His actions, on the whole, support the view that in spite of his position as Duke of Illyria he is young and immature.

Revision questions

The following questions will help with revision.

Questions dealing with general aspects of the play

(1) Coghill has said that, in Shakespeare, marriage is 'an image of happiness that ends his comedies almost as invariably as death ends a tragedy'. With this quotation in mind, discuss the three marriages in *Twelfth Night*.

(2) How important is music (including songs) in the construction of *Twelfth Night*?

(3) What is dramatic irony? Give a number of examples from *Twelfth Night* and comment on their importance in the play.

(4) *Twelfth Night* or *What You Will:* How appropriate do you think the titles of the play are?

(5) Describe the word-play in *Twelfth Night*. Do you find it amusing or effective?

Questions dealing with specific points in the play

(1) How are the main plots introduced in Act I?

(2) Describe the complications that arise in *Twelfth Night* because of Viola's disguise.

(3) What is the significance of the Clown in *Twelfth Night*?

(4) Write an account of Act V showing how the various problems raised in earlier acts are solved.

(5) Describe the confusion that is caused by Sebastian's appearance in Illyria.

Questions dealing with characters

(1) Compare the characters of Viola and Olivia.

(2) Is Malvolio merely a comic character?

(3) What facets of the characters of Olivia, Viola and Malvolio are illustrated by the episode of the ring?

(4) Compare and contrast the characters of Sir Toby Belch and Sir Andrew Aguecheek.

(5) Compare the characters of Duke Orsino and Sebastian.

Part 5

Suggestions for further reading

The text

Most texts of the play have useful notes and commentaries. Two texts which are especially suitable are:
The Arden Shakespeare edition of *Twelfth Night* edited by J.M. Lothian and T.W. Craik, Methuen, London, 1975.
The Penguin Shakespeare edition of *Twelfth Night*, edited by G.B. Harrison, Penguin, Harmondsworth, 1964.

Criticism

The following books should provide valuable stimulation:
BROWN, J.R.: *Shakespeare's Dramatic Style*, Heinemann, London, 1970.
HOTSON, LESLIE: *The First Night of Twelfth Night*, Rupert Hart-Davis, London, 1954.
KING, WALTER: *Twentieth Century Interpretations of Twelfth Night*, Prentice Hall, Englewood Cliffs, New Jersey, 1968.
ONIONS, C.T.: *A Shakespeare Glossary*, (2nd edition), Clarendon Press, Oxford, 1963.
TILLYARD, E.M.W.: *The Elizabethan World Picture*, (A Peregrine Book) Penguin, Harmondsworth, 1963.

The author of these notes

LORETO TODD is a Senior Lecturer in English at the University of Leeds. Educated in Northern Ireland and Leeds she has degrees in English and Linguistics. Dr Todd has taught in England and in West Africa and has lectured in Australia, Papua New Guinea, the United States of America and the Caribbean. Her publications include ten books, among them *Pidgins and Creoles*, 1974; *Tortoise the Trickster*, 1979; *West African Pidgin Folktales*, 1979; *Variety in Contemporary English*, 1980; *Varieties of English around the World*, 1982; and *Modern Englishes*, 1984. She has written a number of articles on varieties of English, Pidgins and Creoles, folk traditions and literary stylistics. She is also the author of York Notes on *The Tempest*, *The Winter's Tale* and *Hamlet*, and the York Handbooks *English Grammar* and *An Introduction to Linguistics*.

York Notes: list of titles

CHINUA ACHEBE
A Man of the People
Arrow of God
Things Fall Apart

EDWARD ALBEE
Who's Afraid of Virginia Woolf?

ELECHI AMADI
The Concubine

ANONYMOUS
Beowulf
Everyman

AYI KWEI ARMAH
The Beautyful Ones Are Not Yet Born

W. H. AUDEN
Selected Poems

JANE AUSTEN
Emma
Mansfield Park
Northanger Abbey
Persuasion
Pride and Prejudice
Sense and Sensibility

HONORÉ DE BALZAC
Le Père Goriot

SAMUEL BECKETT
Waiting for Godot

SAUL BELLOW
Henderson, The Rain King

ARNOLD BENNETT
Anna of the Five Towns
The Card

WILLIAM BLAKE
Songs of Innocence, Songs of Experience

ROBERT BOLT
A Man For All Seasons

HAROLD BRIGHOUSE
Hobson's Choice

ANNE BRONTË
The Tenant of Wildfell Hall

CHARLOTTE BRONTË
Jane Eyre

EMILY BRONTË
Wuthering Heights

ROBERT BROWNING
Men and Women

JOHN BUCHAN
The Thirty-Nine Steps

JOHN BUNYAN
The Pilgrim's Progress

BYRON
Selected Poems

ALBERT CAMUS
L'Etranger (The Outsider)

GEOFFREY CHAUCER
Prologue to the Canterbury Tales
The Clerk's Tale
The Franklin's Tale
The Knight's Tale
The Merchant's Tale
The Miller's Tale
The Nun's Priest's Tale
The Pardoner's Tale
The Wife of Bath's Tale
Troilus and Criseyde

ANTON CHEKOV
The Cherry Orchard

SAMUEL TAYLOR COLERIDGE
Selected Poems

WILKIE COLLINS
The Moonstone

SIR ARTHUR CONAN DOYLE
The Hound of the Baskervilles

WILLIAM CONGREVE
The Way of the World

JOSEPH CONRAD
Heart of Darkness
Lord Jim
Nostromo
The Secret Agent
Victory
Youth and *Typhoon*

STEPHEN CRANE
The Red Badge of Courage

BRUCE DAWE
Selected Poems

WALTER DE LA MARE
Selected Poems

DANIEL DEFOE
A Journal of the Plague Year
Moll Flanders
Robinson Crusoe

CHARLES DICKENS
A Tale of Two Cities
Bleak House
David Copperfield
Dombey and Son
Great Expectations
Hard Times
Little Dorrit
Oliver Twist
Our Mutual Friend
The Pickwick Papers

EMILY DICKINSON
Selected Poems

JOHN DONNE
Selected Poems

JOHN DRYDEN
Selected Poems

GERALD DURRELL
My Family and Other Animals

GEORGE ELIOT
Adam Bede
Middlemarch
Silas Marner
The Mill on the Floss

T. S. ELIOT
Four Quartets
Murder in the Cathedral
Selected Poems
The Cocktail Party
The Waste Land

J. G. FARRELL
The Siege of Krishnapur

GEORGE FARQUHAR
The Beaux Stratagem

WILLIAM FAULKNER
Absalom, Absalom!
The Sound and the Fury

HENRY FIELDING
Joseph Andrews
Tom Jones

F. SCOTT FITZGERALD
Tender is the Night
The Great Gatsby

GUSTAVE FLAUBERT
Madame Bovary

E. M. FORSTER
A Passage to India
Howards End

JOHN FOWLES
The French Lieutenant's Woman

ATHOL FUGARD
Selected Plays

JOHN GALSWORTHY
Strife

MRS GASKELL
North and South

WILLIAM GOLDING
Lord of the Flies
The Spire

OLIVER GOLDSMITH
She Stoops to Conquer
The Vicar of Wakefield

ROBERT GRAVES
Goodbye to All That

GRAHAM GREENE
Brighton Rock
The Heart of the Matter
The Power and the Glory

WILLIS HALL
The Long and the Short and the Tall

THOMAS HARDY
Far from the Madding Crowd
Jude the Obscure
Selected Poems
Tess of the D'Urbervilles
The Mayor of Casterbridge
The Return of the Native
The Trumpet Major
The Woodlanders
Under the Greenwood Tree

L. P. HARTLEY
The Go-Between
The Shrimp and the Anemone

NATHANIEL HAWTHORNE
The Scarlet Letter

SEAMUS HEANEY
Selected Poems

JOSEPH HELLER
Catch-22

ERNEST HEMINGWAY
A Farewell to Arms
For Whom the Bell Tolls
The Old Man and the Sea

GEORGE HERBERT
Selected Poems

HERMANN HESSE
Steppenwolf

BARRY HINES
Kes

HOMER
The Iliad
The Odyssey

ANTHONY HOPE
The Prisoner of Zenda

GERARD MANLEY HOPKINS
Selected Poems

WILLIAM DEAN HOWELLS
The Rise of Silas Lapham

RICHARD HUGHES
A High Wind in Jamaica

TED HUGHES
Selected Poems

THOMAS HUGHES
Tom Brown's Schooldays

ALDOUS HUXLEY
Brave New World

HENRIK IBSEN
A Doll's House
Ghosts

HENRY JAMES
Daisy Miller
The Ambassadors
The Europeans
The Portrait of a Lady
The Turn of the Screw
Washington Square

SAMUEL JOHNSON
Rasselas

BEN JONSON
The Alchemist
Volpone

JAMES JOYCE
A Portrait of the Artist as a Young Man
Dubliners

JOHN KEATS
Selected Poems

RUDYARD KIPLING
Kim

D. H. LAWRENCE
Sons and Lovers
The Rainbow
Women in Love

CAMARA LAYE
L'Enfant Noir

HARPER LEE
To Kill a Mocking-Bird

LAURIE LEE
Cider with Rosie

THOMAS MANN
Tonio Kröger

CHRISTOPHER MARLOWE
Doctor Faustus

ANDREW MARVELL
Selected Poems

W. SOMERSET MAUGHAM
Selected Short Stories

GAVIN MAXWELL
Ring of Bright Water

J. MEADE FALKNER
Moonfleet

HERMAN MELVILLE
Billy Budd
Moby Dick

THOMAS MIDDLETON
Women Beware Women

THOMAS MIDDLETON *and* **WILLIAM ROWLEY**
The Changeling

ARTHUR MILLER
A View from the Bridge
Death of a Salesman
The Crucible

JOHN MILTON
Paradise Lost I & II
Paradise Lost IV & IX
Selected Poems

V. S. NAIPAUL
A House for Mr Biswas

ROBERT O'BRIEN
Z for Zachariah

SEAN O'CASEY
Juno and the Paycock

GABRIEL OKARA
The Voice

EUGENE O'NEILL
Mourning Becomes Electra

GEORGE ORWELL
Animal Farm
Nineteen Eighty-four

JOHN OSBORNE
Look Back in Anger

WILFRED OWEN
Selected Poems

ALAN PATON
Cry, The Beloved Country

THOMAS LOVE PEACOCK
Nightmare Abbey and *Crotchet Castle*

HAROLD PINTER
The Caretaker

PLATO
The Republic

ALEXANDER POPE
Selected Poems

J. B. PRIESTLEY
An Inspector Calls

THOMAS PYNCHON
The Crying of Lot 49

SIR WALTER SCOTT
Ivanhoe
Quentin Durward
The Heart of Midlothian
Waverley

PETER SHAFFER
The Royal Hunt of the Sun

WILLIAM SHAKESPEARE
A Midsummer Night's Dream
Antony and Cleopatra
As You Like It
Coriolanus
Cymbeline
Hamlet
Henry IV Part I
Henry IV Part II
Henry V
Julius Caesar
King Lear
Love's Labour's Lost
Macbeth
Measure for Measure
Much Ado About Nothing
Othello
Richard II
Richard III
Romeo and Juliet
Sonnets
The Merchant of Venice
The Taming of the Shrew
The Tempest
The Winter's Tale
Troilus and Cressida
Twelfth Night

GEORGE BERNARD SHAW
Androcles and the Lion
Arms and the Man
Caesar and Cleopatra
Candida
Major Barbara
Pygmalion
Saint Joan
The Devil's Disciple

MARY SHELLEY
Frankenstein

PERCY BYSSHE SHELLEY
Selected Poems

RICHARD BRINSLEY SHERIDAN
The School for Scandal
The Rivals

R. C. SHERRIFF
Journey's End

WOLE SOYINKA
The Road
Three Short Plays

EDMUND SPENSER
The Faerie Queene (Book I)

JOHN STEINBECK
Of Mice and Men
The Grapes of Wrath
The Pearl

LAURENCE STERNE
A Sentimental Journey
Tristram Shandy

ROBERT LOUIS STEVENSON
Kidnapped
Treasure Island
Dr Jekyll and Mr Hyde

TOM STOPPARD
Professional Foul
Rosencrantz and Guildenstern are Dead

JONATHAN SWIFT
Gulliver's Travels

JOHN MILLINGTON SYNGE
The Playboy of the Western World

TENNYSON
Selected Poems

W. M. THACKERAY
Vanity Fair

DYLAN THOMAS
Under Milk Wood

EDWARD THOMAS
Selected Poems

FLORA THOMPSON
Lark Rise to Candleford

J. R. R. TOLKIEN
The Hobbit
The Lord of the Rings

ANTHONY TROLLOPE
Barchester Towers

MARK TWAIN
Huckleberry Finn
Tom Sawyer

JOHN VANBRUGH
The Relapse

VIRGIL
The Aeneid

VOLTAIRE
Candide

KEITH WATERHOUSE
Billy Liar

EVELYN WAUGH
Decline and Fall

JOHN WEBSTER
The Duchess of Malfi
The White Devil

H. G. WELLS
The History of Mr Polly
The Invisible Man
The War of the Worlds

OSCAR WILDE
The Importance of Being Earnest

THORNTON WILDER
Our Town

TENNESSEE WILLIAMS
The Glass Menagerie

VIRGINIA WOOLF
Mrs Dalloway
To the Lighthouse

WILLIAM WORDSWORTH
Selected Poems

WILLIAM WYCHERLEY
The Country Wife

W. B. YEATS
Selected Poems